A CHEROKEE

FEAST *of* DAYS

VOLUME III

JOYCE
SEQUICHIE HIFLER

DI KA NO HE SGI-DI GO WE LI SGI

(SHE WHO WRITES HER PHILOSOPHY ON PAPER)

COUNCIL OAK BOOKS

San Francisco / Tulsa

A CHEROKEE

FEAST

of DAYS

VOLUME III

MANY MOONS

DAILY MEDITATIONS

Council Oak Books, LLC
1290 Chestnut Street, Ste. 2,
San Francisco, CA 94109
1615 S. Baltimore Avenue, Ste. 3,
Tulsa, OK 74119

ISBN 1-57178-112-9

First edition / First printing.
Printed in Canada.

02 03 04 05 06 07   5 4 3 2 1

The author wishes to acknowledge with deep appreciation the help of the late Mildred Milam Viles, daughter of a Cherokee chief, who supplied American Indian quotations from her extensive library in Claremore, Oklahoma.

Portions of this work have appeared in a different form in the author's nationally syndicated newspaper column, *Think on These Things*, or other names the newspapers may prefer.

The Cherokee words and phrases are phonemic translations from the Cherokee syllabary, which was given to the Cherokee people in about 1821 by Cherokee genius Sequoyah. Several dialects change the pronunciations.

PREFACE

Symbols of the spirit—fragrance, music, and light—
float around us the way our world circles the sun.
The Cherokee sees everything in the round—the
moon, the stars, the curve of the earth—but also
sees so many things connected to the earth as well.
It is all a part of time.

We want more time, we weep for more time,
and we waste what time we have. Moving, moving,
moving, will we never rest? Will we never learn that
the American Indian's moon is a time, a season, a
moment, an hour, a day? The moon comes and
goes, but the Cherokee holds his own time in his
heart. He is never in a rush and he does not say he
will do something when he has more time. The
time is right here and now. Every new minute is a
period of time.

No see in many moons, the Indian is supposed
to have said. I have not seen you in a very long
time. Time—the priceless possession that most of
us think we have in abundance, but even while we
are thinking of it, it melts away. No matter, says the

Indian, there is more here now. It doesn't matter that we have not seen you in a very long time. When the right time comes, we will see each other. If the moon affects the tides, towing them in and pushing them out, it will bring us together again at the right time.

JANUARY

COLD MONTH

UNU LA TA NEE'

JANUARY 1

A new day, a new year, a new era. Many moons have passed and they were not all spent in good pursuits. We spent the time lavishly, we bestowed a profusion of attention on people and circumstances unworthy of our purpose. I am young and have all the time in the world, or I am old now and there's no need to try this late in life.

Youth counts the hours the way Abram counted the stars. The aged bow to these words of Chief Joseph of the Nez Perce: "Hear me my chiefs! I am tired, my heart is sick and sad. From where the sun now stands I will fight no more." But we cannot decide in one moment how many moons we have. The Great Spirit sees our hearts and loves us anyway. We ask permission to do well with this new time and we know we are not alone.

The frog does not drink up the pond in which he lives.

—TETON SIOUX

A new door opens—a new year has begun. This is a very special time, one year passing away, another beginning. All of us are awed by this event. Yet some are worried while others are confident about what has been promised. What do we see? What is on the horizon?

Seeing what is coming is little different from spotting a deer in the woods. Most of the time we look for the entire outline of the deer—from the rack to the flicking tail—and we miss the joy of glimpsing a live deer scampering through the woods. When we know what we are looking for, we focus: a tiny movement, an ear, a white tail held high—any evidence that points to what we are trying to see. But when we do not believe there is even a deer in the woods, we fail to see any evidence and end up jeering at the idea. What do we miss? Everything, simply everything.

Mutants [whites] have something called gravy. They know the truth but it is hidden under the spices of convenience, materialism, insecurity, and fear.

—AUSTRALIAN ABORIGINES

A kettle of hot soup, a cheerful voice, soft music, and a warm fireside. A time *ale-ye-su'* to enjoy. These precious things could be experienced anywhere if the spirit is happy. Those living in a mansion are no more apt to have them than those living in a little hut in the woods. A rich man may want more, but he will not have more joy.

Harmony, a blending of simple things, a simple gratitude for even the smallest things, makes life beautiful. Even if the rain patters on the roof and falls on the fields and in the river, it does not affect harmony that is true and sweet. Relax and let it fall on everything like manna from heaven.

Persevere onward to the place where the Creator dwells in peace. Let not the things of the earth hinder you.

—IROQUOIS CONSTITUTION

The simple things slip by us because we think certain areas, certain times, are supposed to be complicated and that we are not supposed to understand. We short ourselves on wisdom and enjoyment because we don't believe we are equal to them. People deny their natural ability to understand and to take advantage of who they are and what has brought them to this place.

It is no accident that we are here in this place doing this thing; choices were offered to us in the past and we made them. Sometimes we come to a place to learn something, to be given another boost toward fullness of living. But when we stop and accuse ourselves of having no brains and no heart, we blind ourselves to the gifts of life. We let simple, sweet times slide by while we cry for no reason.

The certainty of the Maori is that the giver of life has given to all people, all things.

—MAORI

It only takes one catalogue with pages in bright colors—pictures of phlox and daisies and beds of tulips—to zip a person's vision weeks ahead. Mellow days will be sprinkled among the wintry ones and flocks of robins will fan out in search of territory to nest. Only one hour of seeing color and joy and peace in the mind's eye can bring a flood of hope and eager anticipation.

Seeing everything dark and gloomy gets to be a habit. Like smoke and soot that hovers in industrial areas of old cities, the dark and foreboding throw shadows across the mind. Whatever controls the mind controls the person because thought is the battleground of good and bad. We can circumvent troubling thoughts by giving ourselves pictures that color the mind with bursts of spring color. And it doesn't even have to be spring.

Whatever life's challenges you may face, look to the mountain top.

—TEWA

JANUARY 6

We often come face to face with questions of fairness. What is right—right without question? Whom can we trust to be our champion when life seems to be a game based on personality?

German poet Goethe told us that one man's word is no man's word—therefore we always need to hear both sides. Who is fair enough to hear one side and want to hear the other? Who will speak for justice when we are unsure of ourselves? When there is no freedom to be truthful, there can be no justice. Only fairness and cooperation can bring about an understanding and a desire to make things right.

May the smoke rise like a cloud and carry away with it all the animosities that have risen between us.

—BLACK THUNDER, FOX

JANUARY 7

Don't be so hard on yourself. Self-condemnation is as bad as being indolent and lazy because it is so extreme and unrelenting. Though restraint doesn't always sit well with us, at least it is more gentle and does not tear down the spirit. Recognize who you are—your own best friend. You are not simply an acquaintance. You are not someone you want to insult or hurt, and you certainly are not someone you want to compete with. Instead, you are a person with special qualities and special gifts, which need to be cultivated.

Go back in time and recall where you got in trouble with yourself. Did someone put you down? Whose opinion do you respect—the words of some outsider who has no tact, or the judgment of your own best friend? As time goes on, you will come to know who your true friends are. And you are the best friend of all.

In our sweetness and respose, we can't help but wonder at the anxieties you give yourself.

—GASPESION CHIEF

Please try to be happy. Not just in outer things but in those of the heart. Too many things exist to interfere with outer emotions. Go where you can relax in the knowledge that happiness is something deep in your heart.

Some stretch their hands out to catch the stars and forget the flowers at their feet. We cannot ignore those things nearest us and expect happiness, for happiness is born within. Our hearts contain all the tools for creating happiness. As elusive as it sometimes seems, happiness does exist—and it is closer than we think.

Happiness is not only good in itself, but it is healthful.

—HOPI

A shadow doesn't always show us what causes it. The shadow is a silhouette or a dark outline cast by something standing in the way of light. Frequently it is quite opposite from what it appears to be. A cluster of leaves can throw a shadow that looks like a huge snowflake, but it is not a snowflake at all.

And so it is with chasing a shadow over someone else's reputation. What seems to be fact may not be fact at all, but only appearance—like the shadow of a leaf cluster that looks like a snowflake. Most of the time we would be lost if we had to depend on appearances. We are so sure of what we are seeing that little can change our minds—until truth moves and the shadow does not.

We are true when we look you in the face.

—CHIEF BLACKFOOT, CROW

A path winds through the woods to the pond. Like all paths, it changes directions unexpectedly and joins other paths to meander across wet-weather streams and around steep little hills. Over the years we forget how many times we follow the same paths. We become so accustomed to the turns and twists, most of us could walk with our eyes closed—except for the gnarled plum that grows too close to the path and will trip us if we don't watch carefully. Somewhere deep in our memories are other little paths, little rabbit runs that we walked so often. Plans were made, fears were put aside, tears were shed, and decisions made along those paths.

When we were children, "around the bend" was a long way from home. Even now we sense when we've gone around the bend, when we've strayed too far. But if we live in spirit, we are always near the paths that lead us back to those who wait with open arms.

Toward calm and shady places I am walking on the earth.

—CHIPPEWA SONG

Never respond to the words of a critic. If there is a lesson in what has been said, learn it quickly but give yourself credit for knowing something. Fight the urge to fight. Don't argue with stupidity—it rubs off on you. Know who you are and don't worry about what other people think. Be your own best friend and avoid trouble like poison, which it is. Be steadfast in good times and bad. Tell fear to get lost and let doubt go with it. Always being in the wrong gets to be a habit, whether or not we are wrong. Time is precious—use it wisely.

It is our duty to think and act and speak in such a way that others will always know who we are. When we are our true selves, others will be less likely to criticize us.

I believe much trouble and blood would be saved if we opened our hearts more.

—CHIEF JOSEPH, NEZ PERCE

Every last one of us is in need of a loving hand—not a permissive hand, and not a hand that strikes out, but one that soothes and stops short of clutching. The human condition is a result of disobedience. Every rule has been broken—every law written or unwritten—has been ignored. Imbalances, injustices, broken hearts, and instability are part of the human condition.

Where is the loving hand? It is within us. When we forgive, when we speak kindly, we set ourselves free. We are part of every loving hand. Though the bad may get worse and the good will become better, we decide which—good or bad—we will be.

You must speak straight so that your words may go as sunlight into our hearts.

—CHIEF COCHISE, CHIRICAHUA APACHE

JANUARY 13

Life has a way of pushing us down and standing on us—but only as long as we let it. And we can push back. Don't wait for a miracle—make one!

Recognize the negatives for what they are—experiences, attitudes, actions, and conditions that have no moral or spiritual value. Plenty of negatives surround us, and we need to know how to protect ourselves. Moral and spiritual values help us as we seek miracles in a difficult world. Always remember that a whole untapped Source waits with miracles for us. Trust that Source—and watch for the miracles. They will come—and we can help them come into being by tapping into the Source.

We should pursue the path we believe to be right.

—BLACK HAWK, SAUK

When you are tired of it all and nothing seems worth the time and trouble, remember that you feel that way not because you want less life but because you want *more* of it! Feeling discouraged can be a sign that you want a fuller life, a better quality life.

Everyone has felt sick, left out, overcome by age or bad experience. Though we may feel like we're the only ones who have ever felt this way, we're not. Our challenge is not to give in to despair when we're discouraged. Instead, when we reach out and give to others rather than always expecting to receive from them, we begin to find love and respect—both for others as well as for ourselves. Then our discouragement dwindles and doors open that we didn't even know existed.

If a person fell into icy waters during the winter they took off their clothes and rolled in the snow and rubbed his body with it and got warm. Then they forgot it.

—PRETTY SHIELD, CROW

Happiness can never be a goal, but only the result of having done something to make others happy. If we expect others to make us happy, we probably won't ever experience happiness! We often wait a long time for happiness to come to us, but we need to realize that the possibility of happiness exists right here, right now. It may not come in the form we thought it would or should come, but it may be much, much better. When we let happiness into our hearts, we experience sunlight, hope, and strength sustaining us. We are not only happy—we are content. Peace of mind and contentment are hard to beat in any circumstance. Just relax and let it happen.

All days are God's days.

—SANTEE SIOUX

Quiet souls come in shy people. They learn to guide themselves through hardships and through loneliness; they learn to befriend invisible friends—and from these friendships they learn to be drawn into the light. Indian children cannot bear to be observed, to be called to perform. But when the light falls on them by their choice, they stand in it however uncomfortable they may be.

Whenever any man proves himself by his good life and his knowledge of good things, naturally fitted as a teacher of good things, he shall be recognized by the Lords as a teacher of peace and religion and the people shall hear him.

—IROQUOIS CONSTITUTION

JANUARY 17

It's hard to be a role model. No matter how hard we try to avoid it, each of us is a role model whether we want to be or not. One person said she could serve as a role model for what *not* to do, but does that help anyone—herself included? Why is it so easy for us to tell others—especially children "do as I say and not as I do?" When children sort through experiences looking for guidance to embrace the good, what happens if that guidance isn't there? Some complain that sports figures should be good role models. That may be true—but it's even more important for us to be good role models in our own, close families. When we are, the world around us cannot break down the standard we raise.

It is for you to make something of yourselves and this can only be done while you are young.

—SITTING BULL, SIOUX

Speaking or hearing negative things brings trouble. Even when it begins as a simple comment, the sound echoes in our ears and then goes into the mind. We accept what our minds tell us. So instead of speaking or listening the negative, focus on good, healthy, creative ideas and suggestions. Give yourself good materials—good thoughts, good words, good ideas—to help you build beautiful roads in life. Give yourself fullness and joyfulness in life by first seeing them in your mind's eye, then finding them in everyday events.

I will be cunning as a coyote.

—MANY HORSES, SIOUX

At one time, Sam-cat would come to the kitchen door and loudly demand attention. He didn't always want to be fed. Most of the time he preferred the food he found for himself. But he came to be noticed, to be stroked, and to be talked to—to know that this was home and he was cherished and wanted.

We all want that kind of attention. Having others need us, warm our hearts, and stroke us with their words is like coming home. Even when we're physically hungry and on our way to get something to eat, we can always stop to be greeted, to be acknowledged and loved. Even the aloof and arrogant melt when they are shown they are loved and wanted. Sam-cat proved that—every time he left his hideaway in the barn or the woods to come to the kitchen for love and attention.

Each man is good in the sight of the Great Spirit.

—SITTING BULL, SIOUX

JANUARY 20

Think of all the lovely things—a moment of inner peace, the flash of a cardinal's wings against the dark woods, the sweet cry of a violin, a soft pillow and gentle sleep. These graces help us keep our balance. Small unnoticed things give us peace. They remind us that if there is anything good to think about we should think on these things. They help us forgive the hurts and release the regrets and grief of yesterday. As we turn to the graces and lovely things of life, contentment flows in.

One who knows how to sing and laugh never brews mischief.

—IGLULIK

If you find yourself in a difficult situation, stand firm. Difficulties can shake your foundations, but they don't have to tear down your common sense. The numbness that seems to take over is a safety zone—a place and time to adjust. Don't lie down or roll over, and don't go to pieces. Instead, speak quietly and gently to your own inner person. Tell yourself to take your time in dealing with the situation. Then step aside and observe the overall picture before making any decisions or making any moves. Rev up your spiritual strength and rely on it. Know there is a strength beyond your own. Use it. Making a quality decision in a difficult situation demands full use of your head, heart, and spirit. You can do it—you will overcome the difficulty.

My children, you must take the right course.

—CORNPLANTER, SENECA

JANUARY 22

E ven when we do something satisfactorily, we still want to do it better. There is always a better way. If we keep trying, we know that—sometime, somewhere, somehow—we can do it better, and we will. Persistence, determination, and faith help us do what we couldn't do simply and easily the first time around. It's important to remember that if what we are doing is too easy, our power and creativity begin to wane. Working hard keeps our power and creativity alive. A better way is always there and faith knows where it is. Find your faith and let it enliven your power and creativity. Together they will help you do what you need to do.

The smarter a man is the more he needs God.

—PIMA

He was ancient—or so his young listeners thought. He looked unflinchingly into their faces. He knew he was being tested once more, so he leaned back and remembered the questions of his own youth. From those questions arose the answers that came with the wisdom of living many years. He spoke:

"I will tell you about science."

He pointed one bronze finger straight up, but his gaze was steady on their faces.

"He is the first scientist. He created it with his words."

He told them that anything they could see or touch was created before the earth and the sky. Never think yourself wiser than anyone else. Sometimes it is the slower ones that get the best ideas. Always look and listen and think—that is the key to science or anything worthwhile.

I turn to the Great Spirit's book which is the whole of his creation. You can read a big part of that book if you study nature.

—WALKING BUFFALO, STONEY

JANUARY 24

Light makes our eyes see. Light ends darkness. Light illuminates the mind. The spirit is light. When nothing works and everything sours, turn on the light. You may see what you did not even know was there.

Women have strength and wisdom even they do not recognize—not until the light comes in. And it will, it will. Trust the light.

Today is fair. Tomorrow it may be overcast with clouds.
My words are like the stars that never change.

—CHIEF SEATTLE, SUQUAMISH

JANUARY 25

Don't intentionally hurt another person. Humiliating someone to show your great power only shows your great weakness. Every act must be answered; it must be accounted for and settled. Absolutely no one escapes the judgment, so now is the time to ask forgiveness and to make amends. What we say comes back to us: our own words judge us; our own words condemn us. Those we hurt may move on, but we will pay for our words and actions—we will be, you might say, "hung by our tongue."

The Great Creator has made us of the one blood and of the same soil he made us.

—IROQUOIS CONSTITUTION

JANUARY 26

One of the keys to getting what we want is to be thankful even as we ask. If we can see something, we can do it—but we must acknowledge that we have spiritual help. It is the Spirit who gives us our dream or vision and helps us bring it into being. The Spirit stretches us beyond our present capability to accomplish what we do not think we can do. Expressing our gratitude to the Spirit can turn the key, allowing the door of our dreams to open. If we have the eye to see beyond present circumstances, we should use it, and use it gratefully. Without such vision, not only the dream dies—but the dreamer as well.

What the Great Spirit made and planned, no power on earth can change it.

—HOPI

JANUARY 27

Do not weep, *de tlo ya'sti*, that things happen that are wrong. There was a time when it seemed I mourned for everything—even a clump of grass on the road seemed as if it were a fallen animal. But all that pain was for nothing. If that clump of grass had once been a living thing, it would no longer be cold or hungry or homeless. It would simply have gone back to the great continuum of life.

We grieve for many reasons, but turn from weeping. Darkness is the backside of light. Turn so you can see the light that shines.

Do not grieve. Misfortunes will happen to the wisest and best of men…. Misfortunes do not flourish particularly in our path. They grow everywhere.

—BIG ELK, OMAHA

JANUARY 28

Having something to believe in supports us throughout our lives. Without it, we are like ships in rough waters with nothing to guide us.

When we try to be broadminded and open to everything, we gamble that all the little side streets we take will lead to something worthwhile. But if we have nothing basic in our lives to support us, we simply wander. We must have something to guide us in the dark. We cannot be mental and spiritual nomads all our lives and expect to have something to show for who we are.

Our God talks to us and tells us what to do.

—HOPI

When we do something to excess—whether that be eating, drinking, or anything else—and say we cannot help ourselves, we're just giving an excuse. In reality we simply have not worked on controlling the things that drive us. People and organizations have made millions by telling us they have the answers to our dilemmas. They promise that their pill, book, exercise plan, or whatever will easily solve our problem—or they'll give our money back. Does anyone ever stay with such plans long enough to see it work or have money returned?

We need to look at the issue of control in our lives. Is there anything beyond our control? Yes, there is, but there is nothing beyond the control of the Spirit. If you do not know the Spirit, you cannot know control. Turn to the Spirit, for the Spirit never fails. Let yourself experience the power of the Spirit.

We may quarrel with men sometimes about things on earth, but we never quarrel about the Great Spirit.

—CHIEF JOSEPH, NEZ PERCE

JANUARY 30

We all have the capacity to be many things, good or bad. What is important is what we do with what we have. Complaining only takes up precious time and gains us nothing. Many people make careers of being grossly negative, even though they may have fine opportunities. Others take one small idea and study its possibilities until it becomes an asset that cannot be ignored. Whatever happens to us is the result of what we dwell on—what we think and what we imagine. We are our own designers, engineers, builders, and marketers. None of us is destined to fail—unless we decide we were born to lose.

Once I moved about like the wind.

—GERONIMO, APACHE

Once we have been made to fear something, it is never difficult to be afraid of it again. Such things hang in the back of the mind like an insect caught in a fragment of spider web. Although the same experience may not come again, it is possible that enough of it remains to terrorize us again. Our emotions work in different ways, but fear is the most common and the hardest to get rid of. Fear is a stick that stirs the bubbling brew of all our negative feelings.

Meeting fear takes determination and direct action. Tell it firmly that it is not welcome and that it can no longer distort your thoughts or come into your dreams. We are in charge and must choose what stays and what goes. Fear must go.

My friends, your people have both intellect and heart; you use these to consider in what way you can do the best to live.

—SPOTTED TAIL, SIOUX

FEBRUARY

BONY MONTH

GAGA LU'NEE

FEBRUARY 1

When I see you unexpectedly, it is like having the sun break through heavy clouds to throw gold everywhere. Your welcome smile is like a great big sunflower smiling back the sun. It gives my heart a needed lift.

Never think for a moment that I do not notice your brightness as you come into view. How warm and sweet and sunny you make the world for everyone! My words are a warm hug for you from everyone. Take it, and keep on lifting hearts with your smile.

It seemed as though the flowers were staring at me, and I wanted to ask, "Who made you?"

—TATANKA, SIOUX

FEBRUARY 2

Watch those images you build in your mind. Though some of them can be quite beautiful, some may be dark and dire. We seem to be experts in building negative mental images. Or we can't focus on anything. Something triggers a thought and we are off like a hound chasing something in the deep woods. Then another thought comes along and we chase that for awhile. If we're not like a hound, we're sometimes like a fish—over and over we jump out of the stream to catch an elusive insect. We never catch it, but we keep on trying no matter what.

Try to keep your thoughts focused on things that are worth focusing on! Important thoughts are worth returning to again and again, because on some deep level, they feed our spirits. As Thoreau put it, "Know your own bone, gnaw at it, bury it, unearth it again."

We are like fish in the water, we jump at whatever is thrown.

—MUSCAHTEWISHAH, KICKAPOO

A less than attractive face can smile and we forget the homely features—but we don't forget an ugly temper or an ugly personality. When I was very young, my grandmother would send me to the chicken house to gather eggs. A hen might be on the nest, but I could still slip my hand under her in search of eggs. But sometimes I forgot which hens were just sitting on the nests and which were incubating eggs. If I mistakenly slid my hand into the nest of a brooder hen, she would explode with pecking and squawking. I never forgot it.

Some people are like brooder hens—they have hair triggers that are ready to go off for any reason. At least the hens have a reason for being that way. But life for people like that must be miserable—and their main aim seems to be to make life miserable for others. Don't make war, make peace.

If they [my warriors] are to fight they are too few, if they are to die they are too many.

—HENDRICK, MOHAWK

Cold weather makes sound carry for miles. A dog barks, calves bawl, cows answer, an owl hoots, and you know it is winter in the country. Somewhere in the distance coyotes tune up and our dogs listen intently. It makes a person wonder if domestic dogs and wild ones speak the same language. There may be a siren or a truck horn on a faraway highway where a driver pushes to get over a steep grade. The sounds come clearly, and so do the unusual sounds of birds in the woods—ones we never hear any other time. Farm machinery clangs, doors slam, and so it goes while we listen to other people's lives without their knowing it.

We have a multitude of ways to communicate and let others know they are not alone in the world. But one other thing we always need to remember: let the sound you make be joyful.

The ground says, "It was from me [that] man was made." The Great Spirit, in placing men on earth, desired them to take good care of the ground and to do each other no harm."

—YOUNG CHIEF, CAYUSE

Notice the characteristics of gentle people, those who are not poised to react to every negative situation. They don't sulk or pout, and they truly want to help whenever they can. Gentle people entertain no animosity or feel any glee when someone stumbles. They do not give up on loving and caring deeply—nor is it their nature to push or control. They don't treat others as though they are bugs caught under a glass.

Sometimes we try too hard to be everything to everyone, and it is not possible. Gentle people help where they can, but they do not demand results. They allow peace. They appreciate others who give so much, for so little.

The true human is someone who is aware, someone who is, moment by moment, totally and completely merged with life. He is a listener.

—JOSEPH RAEL, UTE

Sometimes we smile as we remember the fragrance of a flower, the beauty of a sunbeam, the elegance of a strain of music, or the wonder of birdsong in early morning.

How rich we are in memory! What wealth we can cull from what once seemed unimportant! Surely this is all we shall ever need. Good memories dissolve old dead unhappy thoughts. What's left is the "cream," the rich and wonderful memories that feed our hearts and make us smile. What a gift—they are there for us to enjoy over and over in the silence of our own mind.

Waniya, waniya, wakan—*spirit, life, breath, renewal, it means all of that.*

—JOHN (FIRE) LAME DEER, SIOUX

This winter morning offered a nice view in every direction. Beautiful sheep grazed on the east side and a herd of deer, seven does and yearlings, ate acorns on the west side. A deer feeder filled with corn hangs from an oak tree, but the squirrels usually get there first. Tell me there are other beautiful sights in other parts of the world, but this is our land, our woods, and to us nothing compares with it. Most any time of day we can look out and see something that delights our spirits—an owl, a water bird croaking along on the way to the pond, and even a coyote or two. Feeding our spirits is as necessary as feeding our bodies. Good books, music, and sunshine can help us to see and hear afresh. This is what the Cherokee calls "a breaking up of those things that set up in the mind and will not move without coaxing." Time spent enriching the spirit is worth an abundant effort.

To us the earth was tame, was bountiful, and we were surrounded with the blessing of the Great Mystery.

—CHIEF LUTHER STANDING BEAR, LAKOTA

FEBRUARY 8

Every good photographer knows the important thing is focus. Focus is first, and then other things follow. Even so-called candid shots that look spontaneous and turn out to be keepers rely on the steady hand on the camera. Total concentration on a precise moment makes all the difference.

Whatever we want, whatever seems the right thing for us requires focus and dedication. We cannot waver when we are placing our mental images, changing our minds, and beginning all over again. There is nothing wrong with changing our minds. From all appearances, we need to do more of it rather than jumping in with no real direction. But once we find a perfect place, we need to focus steadily and get a clear picture.

What we are living today is what we focused on yesterday. Is it cloudy or blurry? Is the color true? Is the picture true? Or have we distorted the images by not being focused?

A pause giving time for thought was the truly courteous way of beginning and conducting a conversation.

—CHIEF LUTHER STANDING BEAR, LAKOTA

The earth and the world are two different things. A map of the earth shows landmasses and water. A map of the world shows people masses and attitudes and the circumstances surrounding them. The earth has hot spots, geological upheavals, and interaction of the elements. The world has political hot spots, social upheavals, and conflicting attitudes. There are questions about what is wrong and what is right, what is superior and what is inferior—and who is to rule the world. The earth has little wrong—it goes along renewing itself, trying to stay whole and clean despite human tampering. But it is the responsibility of the world to clean up its act as well. Some think it all began when the atom was split, but in all honesty, the real trouble began when man split with his better self. Individual choices are involved here—and whatever we can do to help, we had better get to it.

Everyone makes his feast as he thinks best.

—BLACK HAWK, SAUK

FEBRUARY 10

When we got word that snow was due, our first thought was that it would be a good opportunity to clean out files, closets, drawers, and pantries. Snow fell as though all the geese that ever flew over had discarded their feathers. The great fluffy flakes mesmerized everyone—and all work was put aside. What fun to watch all the birds gather at the feeders. Dozens of tiny finches clustered around a mesh tube of thistle seeds. Just watching was more relaxing than therapy could ever be.

The need to clean up and put things in order is always there, but how often do we get to watch the red birds, blue jays, goldfinches, and snow all at once? Even when we have many things to do, it's good to take time for awe, time for beauty.

When you begin a great work you can't expect to finish it all at once.

—TEEDYUSCUNG, DELAWARE

This is a friend who knows no envy, no jealousy, and has no need to resent you. Knowing and forgiving and supporting you is the real reason for this friendship. Who is this unknown friend who has been hidden too long? This friend is—you! This is the real of you that no one can hurt or taint or find fault with. Trust this one, love this one—know and depend on the real you.

Don't be afraid to cry. It will free your mind of sorrowful thoughts.

—TALAYESVA, HOPI

FEBRUARY 12

Somewhere, sometime, your dream will come true. Your dream, if you have shaped it and given it substance, is sitting in a mental package, ready to come forth. A dream is a vision given to you to work with and to bring into being. If some unfeeling person has told you that dreaming is a waste of time, you waste your time listening to that idea. Anything you can lay your hand on, anything you can see, anything that comes into your head as a good idea, was a dream before it ever happened.

As country children growing up, almost all our activity involved dreams of what we were going to be when we grew up. Those who had no dream let the world decide for them what they would be. A proverb tells us, where the people have no vision— they perish. Give gifts of vision to your children by playing the game of "see yourself as…." Try it yourself.

Treat all men alike…give them a chance to live and grow.

—CHIEF JOSEPH, NEZ PERCE

Right this minute someone has a need and has no idea how to meet it. Right this minute someone feels alone and has no one to tell them they are loved and cherished. Right this minute a child needs reassurance and love and protection from real and imagined enemies. Reach past personal woes and see these people. See these situations and help without calling attention to yourself. Simply do a good deed—for the good, not the glory, of it.

Too little is being done because too many wait for recognition for their good works. Some will not get involved for fear of helping someone who doesn't deserve help. None of us especially deserves love, peace, or other kinds of help, but that doesn't mean we don't need it. We can be glad for the grace of receiving without deserving it—grateful for those who give without measuring the outcome.

What it boils down to—do the right thing.

—YUROK

FEBRUARY 14

It seemed like such a good idea to give an elderly lady a teddy bear. I hoped that it would soften her approach to life and she would feel better. Maybe for a time it did, but in the long run feeling better often means putting aside negative personal attitudes for more positive ones. If you are waiting for that "something" to happen so that you can be happy again, know this: something has happened many times but you did not see it worthy. You must begin to change what needs to be changed. Everything is not going to change to suit us. But we can do something: we can come to know ourselves and why we react the way we do to perfectly harmless events—and then deal with it. No one else can do it, but oh, how it needs to be done.

Love is something we must have. We must have it because our spirits feed upon it.

—CHIEF DAN GEORGE, SALISH

Beauty and ugliness exist in everything—even in some of the same things. We are accused of wearing rose-colored glasses if we see beauty in everyone and in everything. Would it not be hard to see nothing but ugliness? To some, a barren landscape is total emptiness. To others, it is uncluttered simplicity filled with all that is beautiful and serene. Physical appeal is high on some lists, but comfort lasts longer. Whatever is in our hearts is in our sight. To love is to see beauty and life, but never what is wrong. Brooding over ugliness in ourselves or in other people is such a waste. When we are gentle in our observations, we can see and cultivate the best in ourselves and in those around us.

The white man does not scalp the head, they do worse, they poison the heart.

—BLACK HAWK, SAUK

Strength comes by doing. Say you are going to do something in no uncertain terms and you can do it. Some things are simply worth the effort.

When we start saying we are not able—we are not able. If we give up, we give up more than we intend to—and we cannot regain it easily. If we give an inch, life will take a mile. If we let something happen thinking we will make it up, forget it. Now is the time to make the difference, not some future time. Think "GO," and then do it.

I feel grateful to the Great Spirit for strengthening my heart.

—PETALESHARO, PAWNEE

Think before you speak. You may be on foreign ground and cannot see what someone else is truly doing. If you think you heard something, check it out before you begin to accuse. Don't be a pessimist. Refuse to believe in pessimism. If something doesn't come out the way you want, forge ahead. If you think it is going to rain, it will. In other words, we are each the prophet of our own life. What we see and say is the blueprint for what happens from this point forward.

You are fools, you are blind...you have no ears...and you cannot hear.

—WASHAKIE, SHOSHONE

FEBRUARY 18

Check your tongue. Has it been working over-time? Has it been repeating too many things that it should not repeat? The Indian's stoic nature is not particularly silent, but he has learned the import of his words. Don't say it if it is not necessary. Remember, when you talk, the young hear you.

The Great Spirit whispers in my ear, No!

—BLACK HAWK, SAUK

Control is a touchy subject, because it makes us think we can do anything and say anything and no one has a right to challenge us. Control should be bound by friendship—not necessarily with those who are under our control but friendship with ourselves. If people love and respect themselves, they will love and respect others as well. Do good to others, but do good to yourself as well. Stop and think what you must look like to others. Are you overbearing? Is it your nature to get what you want by treading on the feelings of others? Kindness takes only a few minutes, and heals many wounds.

If all would talk and then do what you have done, the sun of peace would shine forever.

—SATANK, KIOWA

Most of us don't like to wait. Waiting is difficult, but sometimes if we do wait, the result can be wonderful. If we simply wait without imagining or expecting or hoping, we are just spending, or wasting, time. But if we wait while imagining success and seeing our hopes being realized, that kind of waiting is a good use of time. During that time, we can decide what we want and then give thanks, joy, and praise to the heavens. We must wait expectantly—anticipating that we will be given that for which we wait. The success of waiting is in our power—we must use it wisely.

We will wait a little while and see what effect your preaching has upon [our neighbors] and if it makes them good, we will consider what you are telling us.

—CHIEF RED JACKET, SENECA

Rest is imperative. If we do not rest, we deplete our power to do, to create, to align our thoughts with the Higher Source. The very young think their strength is unending and that they will always have energy. But if they don't rest, they too become slower, less attentive, and lose their sense of well-being.

The aged fall asleep wherever they are—not because it is wise but because they cannot help themselves. They learn to take their rest whenever they can. When they rest body, mind, and spirit, they are full of potential and full of power—even more so than when they were young. Rest is important—so rest well and rest often.

Hear me, my Chiefs, I am tired.

—CHIEF JOSEPH, NEZ PERCE

Words tattle and turn strength into weakness. Say you won't and you will. Say you will and chances are that you won't. What you say you will do falls short of the truth. Albert Schweitzer put forth the idea that a person has to believe himself capable of thinking truth or he becomes a skeptic. Think deeply, meditate on meaning, look for truth in everything—but watch those words. Many of them have no real purpose and should not be spoken at all.

O be quiet, crow! We hear you.

—ABORIGINAL ELDER

Speak to me of quiet places, of treasures yet to be found, of peace that flows like a river. Tell me of tranquil places that no hand has marred, no storm has scarred. Give me visions of standing in sunlight or feeling spring mist against my cheek. Show me paths that wind through the wild lilies and beds of buttercups. Sing me the songs of the spheres, the mingled voices of wrens and meadow-larks, the lowing of gentle cows and the whinny of the mare talking to her colt. Lead me past the glass-smooth pond where frogs croak of their graduation from frisky tadpoles to squat green frogs that wait patiently for a flying insect. Find me a place in the sun to sit and think and listen to the sweet inner-voice that says so quietly—peace be still.

The earth has always been talking to us, but many of us have lost our sensitivities to sound and vibration, so we do not hear her.

—JOSEPH RAEL, UTE

If you are sick, it is not a feather in your hat; it is a boulder on your path. There is something about an ailment that loves to crown itself king. We have to remember that we are not sick people trying to get well, we are well people fighting off something that is trying to make us sick. Sometimes fighting illness is like standing in quicksand—we work and work and nothing happens.

The danger of having illness is that it makes us feel special. Begin to climb out of that hole by saying this: "I am strong. I am well. I am overcoming this because I have other lovely things I want to do." Don't be afraid of bad germs and incurable illness. Rebuke them. Use your tongue to destroy all the things that are trying your body and your spirit. Montaigne said, "To make a crooked stick straight, bend it the contrary way."

All living creatures and plants derive their life from the sun.

—OKUTE, TETON SIOUX

FEBRUARY 25

The time has finally arrived to have gardens tilled and fields plowed for spring crops. There will be more cold weather, but that is a part of the cultivation of good crops. Freezing causes the soil to mellow and turn soft and pliable. Robins love the plowing. They follow along and pull earthworms out of the soft dirt. Grandfather always chuckled and said they reminded him of old-time preachers in tails and he liked having them following.

Please don't miss the simplicity of little things. They will sustain you when all else fails. When our minds only dwell on things for show, it is such a waste—because "show" won't sustain us when we need comfort and strength.

The roots of a plant go down deep, and the deeper they go the more moisture they find.

—SHOOTER, TETON SIOUX

There they go—all those people rushing and pushing toward something. Do they know something we do not know? Do they see beyond where you and I can see? Should we be doing the same thing? Isn't it funny how people sometimes act so much like farm animals? One cow starts toward the pond and all the others line up behind her. One chicken rushes toward the feed and all the others run in fear of being left without food. Do we know any better than a cow or a chicken?

People have always wanted to be the first to know, the first to do. But when we rush off trying to do what everyone else does, to dress as everyone else does, to eat what everyone else does, we may find ourselves very unsatisfied—because we haven't paid attention to what we really need and what really nourishes us. Pay attention to what really feeds you.

All birds, even those of the same species, are not alike.
—OKUTE, TETON SIOUX

Many of us say we will not believe what we cannot see, but can we see gas or electricity or thunder? We see the results, but we cannot see what we know is real and powerful. Indians often heal themselves with herbs, but they usually do not know how they work. They only know that they do work. They cannot intellectually tell what the combinations do for them. They simply know they heal and it is enough.

Faith is a word that gives people the willies. They think it is some strange thing that removes them from reason, and they never stop to think what faith they put in their car, their telephone, an elevator, the friendship of another person. Faith is looking at the Source and knowing it will not fail. Fear of faith is one of our worst enemies.

Our religion is traditions of our ancestors, the dreams of our old men.

—CHIEF SEATTLE, SUQUAMISH

Some things are not meant to be handled, pawed, or too closely examined. For instance, don't touch a butterfly's wings. Don't take a fawn from its hiding place, and don't caress a woman when she is angry. Delicate is the word. Use the light touch if it is wise to touch at all. Settle down and stop trying to force things. Maybe another person is wrong, but why rub it in? Life runs much more easily when we allow others to arrange their thoughts and actions without too much meddling. Wisdom does not come by force, but by understanding and loving—and, above all else, by keeping our mouths shut.

Before talking of holy things, we prepare ourselves by offerings.

—CHASED-BY-BEARS, SANTEE SIOUX

MARCH

WINDY MONTH

UNU 'LA HEE

MARCH 1

We cannot assume that all good things are ours simply because we have a right to them. The right does not qualify us to get something, but it means the door is open and we can work to achieve our goal. Part of the work is being grateful for the opportunity. But even the opportunity does not do the work—we do it.

Samuel Johnson said that great work is performed, not by strength, but by perseverance. But even opportunity does not do the job. We do. There is little opposition where willingness to work is present. The land is ours, every flower, every bush, it is all ours and we are happy. We will work.

Folly, inactivity, and cowardice? What need we speak of the past?

—TECUMSEH, SHAWNEE

MARCH 2

What happened today that stirred you up and continued to nag long past the event? Have you been dominated by a control freak, or did someone leave the room on a happy note and come back mad as a wet hen? We cannot analyze or make excuses for others, but we can be kind. We can ignore what we know we had nothing to do with and didn't cause. We can carry on as though the world has not changed in the last five minutes.

When someone is angry or hurt or spoiled, they tend to want everyone to pay for it. Don't. It is their problem, and they alone should be smart enough to see how ridiculous it is. Go on with your life, but be alert. Know in your heart and in your spirit that you cannot be put down. Hold tight to your common sense and know you are spiritually protected always.

When you find something bad in the white man's road, drop it, leave it alone.

—SITTING BULL, SIOUX

When life hurts, use your good imagination. See yourself free of pain, physical or emotional. See yourself having a stone lifted off so that you can go free. Then be grateful that you have weapons against whatever it is that hurts you. Your words are your weapons—not words that cut and hurt but words that lift you up and set you free. Say to yourself: no weapon formed against me shall prosper.

Call for new and better circumstances to come in and replace the hard ones you have been dealing with. Words are creative. Don't insist on seeing how they accomplish what they do. Just know they are creative—we cannot use them in wrong ways and expect to get good results. Be kind to yourself. Not indulgent, but simply kind. Coax yourself into peacefulness and pat yourself on the head for no other reason than to stir up your courage. You are worth it—and more, much more.

He pauses in an attitude of worship.

—OHIYESA, DAKOTA

MARCH 4

A time like this one has never before existed. There is swift progress in some areas and feet dragging in others. We wait to see if those things we know are not acceptable will suddenly be right. This never happens. If it is wrong, it is wrong and we know it. The years come and go and lines are drawn, but to what avail? The decision is ours and always has been.

Deep in our spirits we know when some situation leads us down the wrong path. We close our eyes and claim that God is a good God and will not let us go down the drain. But if we insist, he will let us do whatever we choose. If we are ever to overcome, this is the time to change. No greater peace or freedom exists than to get our ducks in a row and to know where we are going and why.

If I thought you were sent by the Creator I might be induced to think you had a right to dispose of me.

—CHIEF JOSEPH, NEZ PERCE

Sheep and goats have to be kept separate. Sheep are mild and graze quietly while goats nip and bite and keep things stirred up and unpleasant. Every teacher is acquainted with sheep and goats. The goats usually outnumber the sheep and they are constantly on the move, doing something to keep others from giving their full attention to what they should be learning. Am I a sheep or a goat? How many times have I disrupted the short time given to learning how to solve problems? Children and adults should know how to be quiet in a public place—how to do our part in making the time pleasant and rewarding. Leaders should never have to be disciplinarians; we behave ourselves because it is the right thing to do. For certain periods of time there should be no unnecessary movements and no excessive noise, even if we have to insist on it.

Silence and isolation is the rule of life for the expectant mother.

—OHIYESA, DAKOTA

Wide prairies and grassy hills are showing a sheen of green in protected places. Then snow begins to spit and grains of sleet show up on the walk. This is spring trying to begin. Time changes with us when we blow hot and cold. We are not precise, we play it by our emotions, and we know how the emotions can waver like a flag in the wind. We prosper greatly when we stop and give thanks any number of times a day. Without gratitude we have difficulty bringing anything new and better into our lives.

Soon the sun will shine more, the flowers will bloom, baby squirrels will play around the nest and our hearts will lift and sing. Such little things deserve to be appreciated because they feed our souls. Spring is on its way and the cold cloudy days will give way to mellow breezes and colors we could not have imagined. The earth and we are of one mind—pause and be renewed.

The earth and myself are of one mind.

—CHIEF JOSEPH, NEZ PERCE

Even though we may not have seen friends for a very long time or even if we live many miles apart, that time and distance mean nothing to friends. We find each other again and again to share all that is important—and a great many things that are not important. Friends know how easy it is to get off center, and they forgive us whether we deserve it or not. But friends also have high expectations for us, maybe even higher than we have for ourselves.

We are at our best when we can be steadfast with other people, when we can make allowances for lapses and do it for no other reason than the fact that we are friends. When we have someone who stands with us in silent communication, that connection becomes a peaceful and long-lasting relationship that never gets old, and never comes to an end. Such a friend is priceless, and being such a friend is a sweet responsibility.

Ancestors handed down our religion…it teaches us to love each other, to be united.

—CHIEF RED JACKET, SENECA

March winds tell us how close the time to plant is getting. They lift up the carpet of leaves on the hillside and send them dancing straight up on end where they land in piles to become compost for the garden. But very often the wind finds them again and moves the heap to a new location until the rains come. We pray for the rain because without the moisture the leaves take a very long time to compost, and the garden will not grow from lack of nutrients. So it is with us—we must be fed if we are to produce. We must have nourishment, mental, physical, and spiritual food or our bodies and souls languish. But the rain will come if we call to it—not all at once but in the right spirit and at the right time.

I never ask for anything that is not needed.

—SITTING BULL, SIOUX

Many watch the heavens to see planes and satellites and things humans have set in orbit. I look for stars and planets and sometimes shooting stars. I see the moon and sun and feel their presence even when there are clouds. As the poet said, "...split the sky in two and let the face of God shine through."

Recently the northern lights, the aurora borealis, rouged the sky with rosy shades. It reminded me of childhood when it had snowed and the northern lights tinted the snow pink—a fairyland that only a child could appreciate to the fullest. We have seen meteorites and comets, and we are promised we'll see more if we will only look up. The promise will be fulfilled.

I am an old woman now...I seem to see our Indian village.

—BUFFALO WOMAN, HIDATSA

A part of success is staying power. What seems to be a remarkable idea on paper may be a colossal failure in practice. This is why we have to be more than what we seem, not worrying about what shows but mustering the power to keep on going when everyone says we cannot. Whether our task is building a house or a business, a bridge or a life, we have to have something to back us up—to keep us going when nothing looks promising. Most losses result from investing ourselves in something that looks good but has no substance. We lose more than we realize by entering into situations thinking that if we don't like it, we can back out later. Strength in any situation lies in seeing things clearly, faults and all. Then when things get to a hard place we know how to handle ourselves. Staying power is having faith in the little things and being willing to change ourselves.

I claim a right to live on my land, and accord you the privilege to live on yours.

—CHIEF JOSEPH, NEZ PERCE

MARCH 11

Thoreau said he once saw a delicate flower growing two feet high between the horse's feet and the wagon track. He said if the plant had grown one inch higher or one inch to the right or to the left, it could not have survived. This flower had flourished without considering its limitations. Like that flower, we can survive in very tight quarters or difficult situations if we have to. At the same time, we may ignore warnings that would be wise to pay attention to. We go on hoping trouble will miss us or go around us. But it's important for us to be prepared for trouble that may come our way. Wisdom teaches us not to wait until the roof leaks to mend it. Do it now.

Our God gives us the rain cloud and the sunshine.

—HOPI

MARCH 12

This morning dew hung in crystal drops along the fence and sparkled in fragile spider webs stretched from grass to small shrubs—a rare glimpse of nature's ornamental skills. Everything glistened in the early morning sunlight. Every plant and bush shows signs of spring, and buds are about to pop. Tiny flowers bloom in sheltered places and a green sheen covers the lawn and touches the trees, which are now ready to leaf out in abundance. We no longer have to endure cold weather, except for an occasional burst of wind and a pellet or two of sleet. This can be called prespring. If we hold on, we will soon enjoy mellow breezes and warm sunshine. Maybe the winter builds endurance in us. Our patience is sure to bring us joy and well-being. Spring will surely come if we wait.

The old Lakota was wise. He knew that man's heart away from nature becomes hard.

—CHIEF LUTHER STANDING BEAR, LAKOTA

The prophet said there is a time for everything under heaven. A time to laugh, a time to cry, a time to live, a time to die. What he did not say is that what we believe about life makes all the difference.

Do we find good reasons to laugh—and not so good reason to cry? Do we see ourselves as losers, or are we equal to any challenge? Do we expect to be slaves, or do we know we are free to choose how we will live our lives? Sure, some people will try to impose certain images on us and try to make us think we are something that we are not, but don't let that happen.

There is a time for everything, but what we think and say and do play a tremendous part in what we get. Even sickness, prosperity, and love come because we make room for them. Remember that how we act, think, and speak chooses much of our destiny.

Look for benefits that last....

—TEN BEARS, COMANCHE

Sometimes a person or a place—at one time our port in stormy times—in our life changes unexpectedly. We took refuge there, but now we must find another place of refuge. To find a new place of refuge, the right place must be in focus before we start. How can we get there if we don't know where we are going? Not knowing is a fact of life at times. But there is an angel to guide us if we watch and listen. The trouble is that most of us think we know everything, and we rely on our own acumen, hoping it will get us through. But many things are hidden from us, and our own understanding is tiny. We must rely on something—and a spiritual something is the only thing we can trust. In the silence of our own spirits, we can seek the answers. If the questions are right, the answers will come.

The Lakota could despise no creature...filled with the essence of the Great Mystery.

—CHIEF LUTHER STANDING BEAR, LAKOTA

MARCH 15

We cannot find peace of mind from some outer source. What we see and hear and feel may help at times, but these things are temporary. The lasting help comes from an inner source. This source is the Life of life. When we have problems, whatever we turn to, whether it be philosophy or psychology or something else, sooner or later we learn we must draw on our own inner resources to solve life's dilemmas. It is the self and the self alone that must handle living. Some fear that if they allow themselves to go deeper, they will lose their freedom. But some of the most threatening and feared circumstances bring the truest answers. Prosperity, good health, companionship all lie before us, and we must develop our faith to step out and claim them.

Grandfather, Great Spirit, once more behold me on earth and lean to hear my feeble voice.

—BLACK ELK, OGLALA SIOUX

MARCH 16

When evening comes and the wind is high in the treetops, we know a change is in the offing. Will it be warm winds or cold? We think we know, but it is hard to tell and we learn to wait and see.

To "wait and see" is a challenge. Sometimes if we wait and see, there are things we won't have to do. During the waiting, they will take care of themselves. But trouble, too, can brew in that time of "wait and see." We must be aware of what can come, remembering that if we expect trouble, it may very well come. But the bad of trouble has no more power than good, so it is important to expect the good—and to put our hands and hearts to the good.

I was praying to the light and to the darkness, to God and to the sun to let me live quietly with my family.
—GERONIMO, APACHE

MARCH 17

Study a problem for a long time before you start talking about it. Once the talk begins, the problem sets its feet and refuses to move. Talk solidifies in a less than helpful way (except when we talk too soon about something we hope will happen). Once we talk about a problem, the talk will bring it about in a concrete way. No one wants to hear how great your pain is—unless you are overcoming it. The only real thing that moves anyone is caring and respect. So care for and respect others, but also care for and respect yourself and your problem.

Even the commonest sticks and stones have spiritual essence.

—LAFLESCHE, OSAGE

No one can hold you back. Others can say and do things that seem to keep you from moving forward, but if your mind and spirit are free and if you see clearly, you can step past those obstacles. There will always be someone who thinks he is in competition with you and will try anything to throw you into the wrong light. Keep your soul clear of it. Stand and watch them hang themselves by their own words—because if you don't respond to them they will get frustrated and try even harder. Let them, for this is their doing and none of yours. Have compassion for such troubled people and then look to your own clear path.

We know the white man does not understand our ways.

—CHIEF SEATTLE, SUQUAMISH

MARCH 19

If we are not striving for any kind of perfection, how can we expect it to come on us? Why should we receive what we do not prepare ourselves to receive? What blocks us from striving for perfection and preparing to receive what is good for us?

Anxious thought and behavior stand in the way of any progress. But how do we deal with our anxiety? Though dealing with anxiety may not be easy, the first step for dealing with it is quite simple: be quiet. Quieting the self with help still the anxiety. Back away from fears of any kind, and reach for the quiet truth that is always behind our fears. Allow yourself to be pleased, to genuinely appreciate the good moments of life, no matter how short. Cooperate and work kindly with others, because doing so opens the door to the beautiful.

The sun and moon look at us, and the ground gives us food.

—CHIEF BLACKFOOT, CROW

Down at the edge of the lake, lapping rolls the clay until it becomes little round balls of stone. Nature does many wondrous things—so many that we begin to ask if this is nature alone at work or is it divinely directed? Questions flood our minds: What makes the deer so lovely and so sensitive to sound? What causes the owl to call at night? Where is the panther that left its huge paw prints on the side of the pond?

We may not receive answers to all our questions, but our wonder—and our wondering—is a gift in itself. The Divine works through nature to remind us that simple remedies will help with our deepest needs: rest, peace of mind, good nutrition, long walks, prayer and forgiving, spells of solitude, and something to love. Keeping it simple is the difficult part, but nature is there to remind us that simplicity and the divine go together.

Now I can eat well, sleep well, and be glad.

—GERONIMO, APACHE

Is someone missing in your life? Where is he or she when you need them? We like to think that everyone must be where we expect them to be, but life doesn't work that way. Each life has a purpose, and the turns and twists of living bring that plan into being. Watch how things move and change and help us achieve what we set out to do—even when someone we think should be there to help us isn't there. Speak to life and tell it what you expect. The spoken word has more power than we realize.

We don't want anyone or anything missing in our lives, and we don't want to be the one missing in someone else's life. Yet we can't always know the path our lives—or the lives of others—will take, and we should not worry about that. We need to remember not to let the world or our worries steal our peace of mind, for we can look for and expect to receive the answers we need. They will come.

I am here by the will of the Great Spirit...my heart is red and sweet...and I know it is sweet because every-thing that passes me by puts out its tongue to me.

—SITTING BULL, SIOUX

MARCH 22

At times we must turn the tide by saying we will have it no other way. Determination changes circumstances more often than we know. That which is good and right deserves determination and consistent effort. Consistent effort can turn even a little decision into great and wonderful change. So be bold: think clearly, listen with your heart, work consistently and with determination. John Dryden said, "Fortune befriends the bold." You see, the bold are determined.

Do not grieve. Misfortunes happen to the best of men.

—BIG ELK, OMAHA

MARCH 23

Whatever our age, a child still lives within us. We are innocent in ways we do not understand—and we find great contentment in having no need to know all and be all. Hope lives in the inner child that is aware and guileless. Befriend this childlike part of yourself. Lean back into this—the most real part of yourself—and pray.

Little things make us who we are: what we say to ourselves in the privacy of our own minds, what we believe about ourselves, and what we see as important. This little child within us is important. We are who we are because of our choices, and some of our smallest choices have the greatest influence. Listen to the child within, and you will be guided well in the choices you make.

All men are made by the same Great Spirit Chief.
—CHIEF JOSEPH, NEZ PERCE

Each day is laid at your feet to form as you will. Certain responsibilities, some of which you would rather avoid, wait for you to handle them. Take care of them quickly and clear the remainder of the day for what you think will be enjoyable. Remember to be grateful—it sets the tone for all activity. Tell those around you that you appreciate them. Include yourself. If we like ourselves, we like all others. When we set the day to be a pleasant one, we are not as apt to overeat or be quarrelsome and testy. Smooth out the wrinkles with the hands of your spirit and always plan for that beautiful something that comes to those who treat life, themselves, and others as good and companionable traveling partners. This is your life, so wrap it up pretty!

Sometimes wait a day between consideration of your problems.

—DIABLO, APACHE

Forgiving someone does not free that person to do a bad thing again, but it does help you remember the good within that person. It also frees you from the chains of resentment you may hold toward that person. The best way to handle any bad situation is to let it go. If you say you cannot forgive, you have not tried. Holding a grudge—that is, withholding forgiveness—breeds bitterness, pain, and the desire to retaliate. When you finally forgive, you will feel tremendous relief. See how it feels to start all over again, free and clear. You will receive an unexpected reward, for the dividend of forgiveness is love—unconditional love.

O the comfort, the inexpressible comfort of feeling safe with a person.

—SHOSHONE

MARCH 26

Our world is in the throes of change. In difficult times, the tongue can get carried away and it can transform our best intentions into something we cannot handle. None of us are capable of handling anything on our own. The wisdom of a Higher Power is needed—and it is available to us if we ask. Learn to cast aside those things that interfere with peace of mind, and speak words that will deliver all of us. We have the power, but we must use it.

When we look into the history of our race, we see some green spots that are pleasing to us. We also find many things that make the heart sad.

—CHIEF JOHN ROSS, CHEROKEE

Stand on the highest spot, E lis i told us, and reach your arms into the sky and worship. Grandmother was specific in her directions, and we followed what she said. She told us not to worship the stars or the moon, but to worship the One God who was unseen but always present. Sometimes, on rough days, our faith slipped, but it always came back. We knew who we were and we knew who he was and is. The rough times reminded us of our weakness and frailty. But we were—and are—never alone.

When I walk my Cherokee land, I feel my grandmother telling me the same things she told me when I was a child. She reminds me never to forget them. I may be one little person but never alone—the One God is always there with me.

My heart is very strong.

—SATANTA, KIOWA

Nothing counts for nothing. We have to plant the seed to see the flower. It is necessary to prime the pump with some of whatever it is that we need. If it is happiness, then make someone else happy. If we are lonely, reach out to the one who needs companionship. If we have a material need, we need to do the best we can to help someone else.

George Eliot once wrote that one must be poor to know the luxury of giving. But one isn't poor who gives with his heart and makes something count for something.

You, whose day it is, make it beautiful.

—NOOTKA

If anyone ever tells you that nothing is perfect, tell him or her that it can be. Nothing can be perfect when you include the whole world and everything in it. But if one little minute can be perfect and if you can get enough minutes together, it will make such a difference.

What helps to make perfect moments? Taking time to see and hear and feel the things that touch the soul. As locusts ring their golden bells, the cuckoo croaks about rain showers, and the titmouse searches for food, open your eyes, your ears, and your heart. Listen well. Then see the startling blue bunting streak through the shadows of the oaks, and when peace begins to settle in, savor the moment. Don't let anyone tell you that it isn't perfect.

Brother, listen to what we say.

—CHIEF RED JACKET, SENECA

MARCH 30

On a particularly cold winter day, Mother came into the kitchen carrying a load of firewood and dropped it in the wood box. Wasn't she tired of such chores? "No," she said, "it keeps me moving and I don't huddle by the fire. Instead I can breathe deeply the cold fresh air." A few minutes passed and she added, "Don't ever resent a certain duty. Sometime, in some way, it pays off and we are the better for it."

When life is too good, we think too highly of ourselves and our blessings.

—FOOLS CROW, LAKOTA

Provoking your own soul is wrong. So what if you failed somewhere along the way? That was then and this is now. Move past self-criticism and be the new person you are today. Doing something wrong is a part of our daily unfolding. No one is perfect, but when you are not perfect, learn something from it. Then give yourself credit for learning. Give yourself credit for wanting to do better. Always seek to learn better ways of living with others—and yourself.

As a child I knew how to give. I have forgotten that grace since I became civilized.

—OHIYESA, DAKOTA

APRIL

FLOWER MONTH

TSI LAW 'NEE

APRIL 1

Change is a way of life—the seasons tell us so. Yet nothing shakes us like change. Though we may expect it and sometimes even want it, more often we dread it. We dread change because we fear it—we do not think change can be for the better. Things happen that we would never have asked for. We respond by saying, "If only I'd done this" or "If only I hadn't done that." We cannot change what has happened, but we can change how we handle it in our own hearts. We may need to forgive ourselves—or we may need to forgive someone else. If someone needs forgiving, forgive, for heaven's sake, forgive. To be free and at ease once again, we need desperately to release the baggage we have been dragging. It is all we can do.

Great Spirit…made the world to change…so birds and animals can move and always have green grass and ripe berries.

—CHIEF FLYING HAWK, OGLALA SIOUX

APRIL 2

Everywhere we look there are yellow flowers—yellow forsythia, yellow jonquils, and yellow daffodils. Long ribbons stretch across the sky as geese make their way north. Sometimes they fly so high we can hardly hear their call, a sound so primitive it stirs the very life of us. Other sounds—the croaking of frogs, the buzzing of night bugs, and the song of the whippoorwill—all give us signs that life goes on. They assure us that we can stop saying that spring "is coming." It is here.

However sad some things are, spring is joy. We realize that spring does not guarantee that we will feel only joy, but we can be thankful that such joy exists. The joy of the Lord is a spring morning when the birds leave the feeders to sing in the woods. Listen closely, because spring brings an important message. Over and over it says: Live!

Out of the Indian approach to existence there came a great freedom—an intense and absorbing love for nature....

—CHIEF LUTHER STANDING BEAR, LAKOTA

APRIL 3

We have to believe that it is possible to have the courage needed to do the impossible. It is easy to be overwhelmed by all there is to do in our lives—and even more overwhelmed by what needs to be done in the world. Courage will help us do what Spirit calls us to do.

Courage doesn't mean not to have fear or not to feel overwhelmed; courage means to act from the heart. If the Spirit lives in our heart, we can move ahead with confidence. There may be no signs that promise better times, but remember they are possible. Depend on that glimmer of inner light and know that those who do the impossible are those who kept going when everyone said it couldn't be done.

We were given food that was rich and sweet to the taste.

—KICKING BIRD, KIOWA

Favorite things: feather pillows, soft socks, old tennies, a rock to sit on to look at the garden of yellow and orange and red, and a warm brown puppy for company. These are little things, simple things, but at heart they are greater than most big events.

Too much distracts our attention from who we are—and what is really important to us. Our favorite little things help us remember who we truly are. They help us remain connected with our basic spiritual nature, which enables us to be authentic, to be ourselves in the best possible way. We cannot afford to be cut off from the inner life, from our spiritual nature, for this is what sustains us through the highs and lows we face each day.

If I am content with little—enough is as good as a feast.

—NELLIE SEQUICHIE, CHEROKEE

APRIL 5

Spells of melancholy can reflect a need to express ourselves in a better way, a need to branch out in new areas and more fully develop the mind and spirit. When you feel stymied, pent up, confined and limited, fear creeps in and says, "This is all there is or will be." Not so. Take heart! This is where things begin to change. Our eyes may see only so far, but our spirits see forever. This is called "vision." With it, we thrive. Without it, we perish.

Never, never, let self-pity dog you. Never let shadows dominate your vision. Sit in the light of your own spirit and see what is good, see what makes you happy. Reject negative thinking, and make your own happiness.

A good heart and a good mind—these are needed to be a good chief.

—ONODAGA ELDER

APRIL 6

If you have done something wrong, it is right to be sorry. It is right to feel remorse. If possible, make amends, even if it is only to express sorrow. After you have done these things, don't let anything cling to you that says you must continue to feel guilt and remorse. The negatives of life will try to distract you and lead you down the wrong path. Take charge and strive to do what is right. Guard your mouth, even if you have to force yourself to be totally quiet for long periods. No one is perfect, but strive to overcome the desire to hurt and put others down. Remember that what we do comes back to us like an echo in a deep canyon.

The Creator made us to learn by trial and error.

—MOHICAN ELDER

APRIL 7

If you are looking for Utopia, don't move: you may be in it. If something is working well, don't get up and fly off where things do not work well. We dream that if this is good, think how much better it must be "over there." Stay put until there is reason to move around and change things. Changing things is sometimes like helping a baby chicken break out of an eggshell. Sure we can do it, but the chicken needs to do it himself for his own strength. By interfering, we put it in jeopardy. You may be standing on the edge of something truly great, but your need to fling caution to the wind takes you right out of the greatest thing you could do.

Stand still and see. Have the strength and fortitude to hold the line. You may be a big fish in a little pond, but go ahead and swim there until it is clear that it is time to move elsewhere. If you move when you are truly ready, you will thrive—instead of drown—in a bigger pond.

We are content to preserve what we already have.

—TECUMSEH, SHAWNEE

APRIL 8

My dear friend, rise up from being depressed. Circumstances have caused this predicament to last long enough. Stand up and shine! Feel the light deep in your mind, will, and emotion. Let the light flow all through you so that it can burn out the mists and fog that have hidden you from reality. Whatever the day may bring you, whatever hurts or disappointments you feel, search all closely and you will find the strength to counter them face to face. Make this day one of knowing there is no power, no critic, no trouble that can come against your inner strength and your outer calm. Even when darkness seems to cover the world and all its tangled affairs, your light will never go out or let you down.

Observation is certain to have its rewards.

—CHIEF LUTHER STANDING BEAR, LAKOTA

APRIL 9

Forgiving sets us free. This does not mean approving of what we have forgiven. But forgiveness means walking away as free as the wind. Cut the tie that binds. We cannot hold someone else's feet to the fire without burning our own fingers. We must forgive others and put their wrongdoing behind us. That is the first step toward healing.

The Indian has more sense than the white man....
Two objections to a duel: Lest I hurt you and lest you
should hurt me.

—KAHKEWAQUONABY, OJIBWAY

APRIL 10

So much is taken for granted that when change comes, it startles the calmest soul. If the little ordinary jobs seem tedious and unrewarding, it is because we do not realize how the small colorful pieces fit together to make the bright, happy quilt of life.

Focus on the possibility of a new opportunity, a chance to break out of the limited and rigid ways in which we have thought and lived. Now is the time to be open and receptive to the possibilities hidden behind things that seem small.

The white man knows how to make everything, but he does not know how to distribute it.

—SITTING BULL, SIOUX

APRIL 11

Jesus spoke the words to the storm and it was stilled. This is the season for spring storms, and we need to be alert. If we know what is about to happen, we too, can speak the words. Those words are "Peace, be still." Peace can be spoken to one's own spirit, and all the fears that swirl around us can be stilled.

Unfortunately most people speak the opposite of peace. As a young girl I was in a storm cellar with an old lady who told us all the gory details of past storms. She said she knew someone who was sucked out of a storm cellar and never found. Don't listen to the doomsayers. Rebuke the ones who counter peace and stillness, just as you would any storm.

Peace, be still.

—JESUS

APRIL 12

What has the moon got to do with anything, including romantic notions? More than we can know. I was proud of my beautiful green garden with straight rows of vegetables growing—I thought I could grow anything I wished. The beautiful green rows proved to be just that—no root vegetables, no beets, potatoes, radishes—just little wisps of roots for all the work. Then an old Indian told me to plant my root vegetables in the dark of the moon. Why? No idea, but he was right.

Little things count—and sometimes wisdom is so simple that we don't want to pay attention to it. Often we ignore the truth and wisdom of simple people; we feel truth can come only from someone famous, a great orator, or maybe someone on TV. Instead, listen to those who carefully observe the world around them, who know how the moon affects growing plants, who seek the Spirit in every little, living thing.

God made roots and berries to gather, and the Indians grew and multiplied as a people.

—MENINOCK, YAKIMA

Not everyone sees a friend as a wonderful responsibility. Some talk about others freely and self-servingly. When they're with one person, they run another person down. Later they'll switch sides if it serves a purpose. Watch out for those who are envious, the ones who find fault and try to raise their self-esteem by lowering someone else's. The people who act in these ways are not really friends.

True friendship does not come apart at the seams when a strain is put on it. A sweet long-enduring friend is someone you recognize from a long way off—a kinship that reaches past barriers and leaps over differences. Friends may not always agree, but they will defend each other with fervent loyalty. They give of themselves and are grateful that true friendship lasts a lifetime.

Keep from quarreling, live peaceably, and don't say bad things about each other.

—CHIPPEWA

APRIL 14

Don't believe anything you hear, and believe only half of what you see," Grandmother used to say. Hearsay is gossip pure and simple. It can ruin relationships—and lives. Cherokees have always believed that those who carry tales are best left to the judgment of the Great Spirit.

The tongue seems so little and harmless, but like a lighted match tossed into a pile of tinder, the tongue can loose careless words that catch fire and burn out of control. Instead of using it for relaying gossip, use the tongue as a way of expressing love and respect. Our words reflect the kind of person we are. What kind of person do your words say you are?

So they said and he said, and it was that way.

—HANDSOME LAKE, SENECA

APRIL 15

One Indian elder told me, "Never think too highly of yourself." But he went on to say that when you have the right stuff, you know it. You feel secure because you know you're in command of yourself wherever you are. It is not as important to control others as it is to control yourself; what you tell others is not as important as what you tell yourself. If you are due glory, it will come to you.

Never think too highly of yourself.

—TECUMSEH, SHAWNEE

APRIL 16

There is a perfect place in the garden. Tiny, blue-bellied lizards clean up the less desirable bugs and an occasional armadillo lumbers through. Goldfinches swing on tall stems of purple foxglove and bee balm entertains many butterflies and hummingbirds. Even with bits of crabgrass and invasive herbs, it is perfect there.

The garden is perfect because it inspires peace. Perfection exists in this life. As unlikely as it seems at times, the more we fill our hearts and minds with what is beautiful, the more it crowds out anything that is bent on destroying us. If there is anything good to think about, think on these things.

It became apparent in early life that he [Indian boy] must accustom himself to rove alone.

—OHIYESA, DAKOTA

If you do not like what you are seeing now, only wait a minute. Change is inevitable. It comes whether we are ready or not. The fact that it comes so unexpectedly means we need to know where our feet are on the path of life.

But most people don't know where they are— and many do not care. Because they don't know and don't care where they are, they will be even more vulnerable to the challenges of change. When we know where we stand at the moment, our lives are in balance. When it is time for change, time to take the next step, we will be able to take that step and not lose our balance.

Only in quiet waters things mirror themselves undistorted. Only in a quiet mind is adequate perception of the world.

—MARGOLIS

APRIL 18

Go outside, remove your shoes, and put your bare feet on the ground. Close your eyes and feel the difference. Somewhere deep inside something changes, and we experience a sense of well-being. Lean against a tree and catch the scent of wild plum blossoms. Hear the birds sing and the frogs croak. Expose yourself to freedom. Breathe deep and let your spirit soar.

It is the general belief of the Indians that after a man dies his spirit still lives.

—CHASED-BY-BEARS, SANTEE SIOUX

APRIL 19

You cannot rise above what you allow yourself to think or say. If you think you are limited and you say so, then that is the way it is. It is impossible to talk one way and have things another.

You form your life word by word, thought by thought. If things are not the way you want them, then change. A little listening and keeping score on yourself will tell you what your thoughts are and how your words work. Stray thoughts will come in, you can count on it. But mark them down as stray and let them go out again. But be honest in marking what is yours. Pull bad thoughts out like weeds.

When people live far from the scenes of the Great Spirit's making, it's easy for them to forget his laws.

—WALKING BUFFALO, STONEY

APRIL 20

Lois is a dear cousin who has met some tigers on her path and defeated them all. She has a built-in sense of humor, which is as much a part of her as her breathing. When she was ailing, she spent some time lying on the couch, but she said there was a fragment of a cobweb overhead that provoked her every time she looked up. When she was asked if she got up and swept it down, she said, "Oh no, I got up and turned off the light."

A remedy for every problem is available to us—and turning off the light we shine on problems may be the answer. When something is wrong, we keep it where we can see it and that makes it last a very long time. But when something diverts our attention, nine times out of ten the original irritation fades and we never quite get back to it. Divert your attention. Look at something right and see how quickly it absorbs the mind.

It is above that you and I shall go, along the flowery trail…picking flowers on our way.

—WINTU

Always be cautious about taking away hope from another person—or even from yourself. Hope is the substance from which dreams are made. When you can't seem to do anything else, go on hoping. Hope helps you get to the next stage of life. Adults sometimes take away hope from their children. They do that not out of cruelty or mean-spiritedness, but because they fear that their children will be disappointed.

Disappointment cannot compare with hope. We are all disappointed at times, but if we keep hoping, the disappointment fades and a new vision takes its place. Vision is a part of hope—being able to see beyond the impossible and head in that direction even when someone says you don't have what it takes to get there. Yes, you do. Keep your vision alive—keep hoping and moving in the direction the Spirit leads you.

Sing your song looking up at the sky.

—A BLIND NOOTKA WOMAN

APRIL 22

When you walk out into the misty rain, don't think about the mud under your feet—think how softly the rain is falling. In every situation, see the good and speak of it. Mud is so much better than hard dry ground where nothing will grow. So what if the mud gets on your shoes, as long as blessings are on your head?

Talk to everything in your life. You have power to change even the inanimate, the things that seem dead to you. Speak to the rock. Talk to the mountain. Tell your own negative fears to get lost. Talking to yourself is very precious and valuable. But always remember to speak to everything—the rocks, the trees, and even yourself—with love.

We fly over the sky, our voice is light, we make a road for the Spirit.

—PASSAMAQUODY

APRIL 23

Last night the wind changed from warm southern gusts to colder air from the north. High winds swished the treetops and pounded hail against the windows. Eventually the hail became rain, a half inch or so, before everything quieted and the cold front moved through. Darkness fell. Then the full moon peeked out from behind thinning clouds, and fireflies twinkled and winked among the new green leaves of the massive oaks.

We often go through a similar process in the storms of life. Circumstances blow unbearably and rattle the windows of our soul. Harshness, like hail, bombards us and sometimes leaves us broken in heart and spirit. Eventually the storm passes and calm permeates us. Then the beautiful fireflies of hope and wonder return—and life sparkles anew.

The Indian loved to worship. From birth to death he revered his surroundings.

—CHIEF LUTHER STANDING BEAR, LAKOTA

Wisdom is available to everyone, though not everyone is open to it. It is so easy to believe we are failures and not smart enough or worthy of wisdom. But those false beliefs are the very things that hold us back from doing what we have always dreamed of doing. We clutter our thinking with resentment and envy, rather than learning to develop self-understanding. When we finally realize that our destructive thinking makes us our own worst enemy, we can then begin to move past the roadblocks in our lives. As we move freely down the road of life, we can finally begin to do what we've always dreamed of doing.

I know how hard it is for youth to listen to the voice of age. The old blood creeps with the snail, but the young blood leaps with the torrent.

—WASHAKIE, SHOSHONE

APRIL 25

Life shifts us into neutral sometimes. Our engines idle, and our eyes and hearts adjust to the slower RPMs. We hang suspended for a while—waiting. Though we don't know it, often we are waiting for a new vision to emerge—and we must be quiet enough, calm enough to sense its approach. Vision is the art of seeing things that are yet to appear. With vision comes a responsibility like none other—for once we have been given vision, we must seek to bring it into being. Waiting—as hard as it can be—helps prepare us for what is yet to come.

There is an ancient saying that a confused state is that state in which the idea has not yet begun to sing its song of identity.

—JOSEPH RAEL, UTE

APRIL 26

Gardening keeps us close to the earth. When we are good planters and good caretakers, we see results—not once, but many times and in many ways. The garden we walk in more than any other is the one closest to us—the garden of our minds. What are we planting there? What we hear, what we read, what we say—these all plant ideas in our minds. Every area of life reflects the beautiful colors and fragrances of what we think and talk about—because our words plant flowers or weeds. What will you plant today?

Watch your words, they will come true.

—E LIS I, ESSIE SEQUICHIE, CHEROKEE

APRIL 27

The Indians say that when the chief gets too carried away with his position, he may go to sleep one night and wake up the next morning with his entire tribe gone. The moral: don't press your luck, because Indians don't wait for a term to expire. This is not to say that Indians are picky; they just don't waste any time getting things right. If it has to be done, do it. Better no chief than a bad one. The tribe can rule itself until a true leader comes along.

No one is above anyone else. We must always consider the good of others and think about how we can help them find it. If we don't, we may soon be like that chief: we won't have anyone around to listen to us. We'll be on our own. Just as a chief is not much of a chief without a tribe, neither are we much of a person without a community.

Leading us safely, keeping us safe, teach us to be like you.

—PAWNEE

APRIL 28

The woodland path is secluded and beautiful, but it is not the easiest place to walk. No stepping stones pave the path and nothing makes the pace smooth and even. But the rewards are so great I am willing to step over deep cushions of moss and fallen sticks and acorns that are like rocks to the soles.

Trumpet vines have grown tall and now hang so low that I have to bend to walk under them. The cypress is huge and its roots stick out of the ground like children's pink knees. A wet-weather branch of a stream comes down from the hills and is too deep to step into but narrow enough to jump over.

Walking the path is a little like living—we must bend, step carefully, and watch out for overeager dogs that bump and push—but it is well worth the effort and the reward: great peace of mind.

She taught me to kneel and pray to Usen for strength, health, wisdom, and protection.

—GERONIMO, APACHE

APRIL 29

Trouble troubles every person who listens to it. Think of it this way: if trouble has troubled you at every turn, you must be in the process of getting to a new and higher level. Have there been signs of descending or ascending? Are you higher now than five years ago?

Look at what obstacles you have overcome— not without tears and not without stress, of course. But you can turn stress into victory by taking another step upward. Soon you will see the sunrise before anyone else can.

We return thanks to the moon and stars, which have given us their light when the sun was gone.

—IROQUOIS

APRIL 30

When something doesn't seem possible, it may well be that our vision is off center. What we cannot see—can't see, that is, with the inner eye—we cannot understand. Nothing happens without our seeing with inner vision. Nothing can happen without our acknowledging the possibility of inner vision.

However intelligent we may be, however clever and experienced, there exists a world of things we know nothing about. Yet if we are open to our inner vision, we may suddenly come to understand something that we could not understand before. So be open to your inner vision, open to the possibility of your most desired dream coming true. Talk with your inner vision. Invite it to come in more clearly—and then expect something wonderful to happen!

We should understand that all things are the works of the Great Spirit.

—BLACK ELK, OGLALA SIOUX

MAY

PLANTING MONTH

ANA-SKU'TEE

MAY 1

The woods are dense and colored in many shades of green. So many plants zipped through the blooming stage that perhaps they've given the foliage more energy and power. Because the foliage is so thick, everything is covered up and hidden. As a result, even the wild animals wander into strange territory.

Last night I was sitting outside to watch the cats eat their late evening snack. All three were eating at their individual dishes when another one brushed my knee. I thought, "I don't have a cat that color." But this wasn't a cat—it was a raccoon! Both of us were surprised, but neither was scared. He lingered for a long time to see if the cats might leave a bit of food, but his wait was fruitless. I went to bed, the cats went on their nocturnal prowl, and the raccoon headed home to the woods. That is the country way.

Outwardly, the stone is not beautiful but it is solid, like a solid house in which one may dwell safely.

—CHASED-BY-BEARS, SANTEE SIOUX

MAY 2

Giving up and saying there is no use in going on is how the world thinks and acts. But inside each of us is a reserve of strength we have no knowledge of until we tap it. When life gets rough, it is time to turn off the world and its "expert" authority. If we listen, we succumb to the words of the world. What we tell ourselves builds and heals—or destroys. That alone is reason enough to see the power of being positive and the destructiveness of being negative. Which way will you choose?

I would have been pleased if you had never made promises, than that you made them and never performed them.

—SHINGUACONSE

MAY 3

You have power over trouble. Don't let anyone tell you that you are helpless. Like an illness that tries to get back in after you have improved, trouble of any kind will come back much stronger if you give it half a chance. How do we stop trouble? With our words. More than likely our words had something to do with trouble getting a foothold in the first place. Trouble is a mountain—and you can speak to the mountain and tell it to be thrown into the sea. If you work at it, it will happen. Don't expect one saying to do the job—though it often does. Keep on saying what you want to be gone and replace it with what you do want. Never leave a vacancy.

When trouble hits, hit it back with words right from the start. Declare your power to overcome—not with wishy-washy words, but with full determination—and find someone strong to agree with you. And don't forget to say thanks.

Guard your tongue in youth, and in age you may mature a thought that will be of service to your people.

—CHIEF WABASHAW, DAKOTA

MAY 4

In the quiet of the midnight hour, fear will assail you if you let it. All your daytime determination fades in the darkness. Fear says, "Look how vulnerable you are." Yes, but you can throw fear off and refuse any suggestion that you are defenseless. Turn back the dark negatives that parade by you every minute. Tell them they are not acceptable.

You are a different person now. Turn away from anything you may have done wrong. We have all made mistakes, but there is no reason to carry them like rocks on our shoulders. Be the new person that has asked to be forgiven. Show your new colors and you will be supported. Feel fear melt away at your command—and keep on commanding it to obey you. It is your right to profit, to increase, to heal, to be happy—all gifts that you have not opened, all the peace and gratitude for being who you are. Look about you and see your wonderful world restored.

I will sing you to safety.

—AUSTRALIAN ABORIGINAL ELDER

MAY 5

Ignorance is the night of the mind without moonlight or even a star to guide us. Then, little by little, the daylight breaks and we see more clearly. We blink our eyes and feel our way along slowly for a time. As we grow accustomed to being able to see where we are going and what we should do, we are grateful. We stood too long in the darkness; as we move into the light, now is the time to increase in wisdom.

Coming out of the darkness is not easy. We must be careful not to rush back into something that is familiar but not helpful. This is a new day and we must walk in it with caution. We must test and choose carefully, and know our private moments of joy. Slowly but surely our personal identity emerges from the darkness. We must guard it gently and carefully until we see that we are not alone in our walk toward light and wisdom. The Spirit is with us.

My heart is filled with joy when I see you here, as the brook fills with water when the snow melts in the spring....

—TEN BEARS, COMANCHE

MAY 6

New spring growth fills every empty space with grasses, vines, and wild roses. Blackberry bushes have sprung up everywhere and even the lilacs have a multitude of tiny seedlings taking space near the asparagus beds. Nature and human nature seem not to tolerate an empty space. Human nature, especially, works nervously trying to fill this spot and that spot with something—sometimes with whatever is available. Availability seems to be the key.

But we should never settle for something simply because it is nearby. So much that has been ill chosen in life is simply a filler rather than something carefully chosen to be a thing of joy. We should never settle for comfort alone. Caring, intelligent, people grow—and sometimes grow away from—a convenient choice. The empty spot then becomes a mark of maturity. Looking good is not enough—it is being good that counts—not just for now but in all the changing years to come.

Each man is good in his sight. It is not necessary for eagles to be crows.

—SITTING BULL, SIOUX

We short ourselves when we think we do not have time for the little things. After all, the big things are made of the small. Even taking one sunbeam, one drop of rain, one tiny flower for granted can leave a void hundreds of times bigger. Time is important, but we waste it when we believe another person is less important than time itself and therefore not worthy of our attention.

Spend every waking moment being grateful, being kind, being thoughtful. It takes so little to help where we can and to keep our opinions to ourselves unless asked. When we think others are our friends or potential friends, we are walking in grace. We need it just as we need the wonder of every little thing.

Speak straight and your words will go into our hearts like sunlight.

—LIKE IRONWEED, CHIRICAHUA APACHE

MAY 8

Ten minutes can change the world. Why do we think we cannot buck the system? The only thing we cannot change is the spiritual. If there is something we want to do or to change, and it is in keeping with spiritual laws, then we can do it. We need to know we can change the situation. Where human knowledge and expertise leaves off there is a higher knowledge.

Whatever we perceive we can receive. If we can form an image in our imagination—a good image—then it is entirely possible. If it is a wrong image, don't try to justify it. You can't. Never be so stiff-necked that you cannot change your mind and change your life. We all can.

Everything the power of the world does, is done in a circle.

—BLACK ELK, OGLALA SIOUX

MAY 9

It seems early for the whippoorwill to be singing, but it doesn't ask anyone, it just sings when it wants to. Its plaintive song fills the woods in late evening and then the owl hoots—a nice duet. Twilight brings a multitude of sounds and songs and scents. The screech owl can scare the daylights out of a person or it can ripple notes across the woods so sweet it almost hurts to listen.

Primitive and breathtaking, life moves from one place to another, always keeping the soul and the body connected. Life asks if what you are striving for is worth the effort: does it allow you to reach back and touch creation and lean forward and see tomorrow? If someone asks what should they do, ask if they are standing on holy ground. Can they see with the human spirit? Can they love?

Start listening to the silence that is so full of wisdom. Listen to the beauty of bird songs. Drop the brassy facade and develop the person you really are. That is a person worth knowing.

It was the wind that gave them life.

—NAVAJO

C ompetition is a subtle thing. It makes people feel smaller than they really are and it sets up barriers between those who could be true friends. As long as we compete, we cannot be true to anyone—even ourselves. Does anyone care how much money you have or how often you polish your silver? Does anyone want to know how many important people you know? What they really want to know is whether or not you can be trusted—not with deep secrets but with the homeliest of things that are the foundation for friendship.

Don't try to compete—except with yourself. Improve something every day, though it may not show. Be kind and gentle with those who do not seem to need it, because they do. Everyone does.

In order to honor Him I must honor His works in nature.

—TATANKA, SIOUX

Once a teacher told me there is no devil. Is there no evil either? Can I rely on that bit of information? I believed the teacher until I saw evil and I knew it was not from God. Where did it come from? Listen, anyone who teaches there are no opposites is trying to offset the thing that makes them do wrong. Right and wrong, left and right, up and down. There is no void at the opposite end of goodness. It is bad and bad comes from you know who.

If there is anything in your life that has gone wrong, you have to know it came from an evil place. Stop denying your own common sense. We are taught to rebuke evil. If it doesn't exist, how can we rebuke it? Turn away from studying what intellectual man has to say and read the Truth. It will reward you abundantly.

We believe that the Spirit pervades all creation.

—OHIYESA, DAKOTA

MAY 12

Here's some everyday wisdom: dig down into the deepest part of what you know and give it color and shape. Don't even pretend to be intellectual. Talk with simple and comforting words, with plain, everyday language that people of every culture can understand. Talk directly to people, not down to them or looking up. Point the way as you know it.

Stop mulling over what others are thinking and remember the times you needed help. Let it go and be yourself. Pretension is the first sign of insecurity. If self needs to be corrected, you do it—don't let someone else try to do it for you. If someone else fails, they have to fix it. If we fail, it is our responsibility.

When I look upon you, I know you are all big chiefs.

—SATANTA, KIOWA

MAY 13

Remembering can be painful and sometimes without any benefit. Too often we remember and feel guilty because we were not perfect. We spend so much time regretting things that bad memories overshadow good ones. It is easy enough to forget the good things that have happened without covering them with bad memories.

As we look back, we know that nothing was really perfect even though we wanted it to be. We worried and fretted, and some things happened that made us mad enough to fight. It is good that we put away those memories. Stop dwelling on what went wrong in the past. Cut those thoughts loose and live a new life. Time grows more and more precious, and what we do with it at this very moment makes or breaks our tomorrows.

Know things in nature, talk to the tornado, talk to the thunder.

—NAVAJO

MAY 14

If you are a mother or even a stand-in mother, you wonder how you are performing this important job. What are the children doing, what are they thinking, what words are they using? The best we can do is teach, pray, and trust. We recall vividly what our mothers taught us. Mine taught with humor and sometimes a switch. The love was certain and sure—not just for one child but with all children. She could take the sting out of hurt and take away our fear. Mother had a practical view of things. When the kitchen curtains caught on fire, she said not to call the fire department, they would just mess up the kitchen. She wouldn't let us throw water on the hot stove because it would warp. She simply took a blanket and pressed it against the burning curtains after she turned off the source of the fire. It was over in minutes. The curtains never made a comeback, but Mom did. She always did.

It is well to be good to women in the strength of our manhood because we must sit under their hands at both ends of our lives.

—HE DOG, OGLALA

MAY 15

What do we expect? To know makes a difference. We must have a vision or a picture of what we expect. If we do not, life will give us what it has—good or bad. If we watch someone else who is not well, who is needy and unhappy, and believe what they are doing will probably come to us, we are inviting trouble. We need to begin now to act as if we are well and happy. We must learn to expect good the same way we unconsciously expect trouble. It is one or the other—our choice. Like a plant fertilized and given light, we will bloom with a little help.

There is One that made all this, who shows us everything.

—YUKI

Use the thing at hand to get things done. Don't wait for the miracle of the helping hand. Your hand is the helping hand. Don't dwell on the idea that you have to win a lottery to be wealthy. Wealth is so much more than a ton of money. Simply, what do you believe? Not lovable? Show someone kindness and make others know they are important. Not handsome? The most beautiful people are those who are not arrogant and who never try to impress anyone with their importance and take-charge attitudes.

Start here and now being kind—to yourself as well as others. Kindness to oneself is not spending money, not eating and drinking the wrong things, not believing that smoking keeps you thin. Trouble lurks close by and tells us we cannot help ourselves. Yes, we can! Challenge yourself to overcome one thing and three will disappear. Simplify, and see the truth of things.

Take away all arrogance and hatred which separates us from our brothers.

—CHEROKEE

These are the days when purple violets cluster on damp creek banks and wild strawberries put out runners for new plants. This is the time when you can look into a huge green tree and see leaves that have never before existed. Everything is smothered in green, everything is blooming in yellow, purple, pink, and rose. All this will pass you by if you don't look at it. Stand still and see. If you cannot feel better after looking, you have some things to settle. Stop the resentment, stand away from the pitiful self, and rise out of the ashes. Look at the hills covered with sunshine, see the misty curtain that swallows the valley. It is spring and life is as fresh as the newborn calf or the colt that frolics in the field. Stop the fretting and enjoy simply for the sake of your mind and body. Primroses are blooming in the fields and life is good if you will let it be good.

A big man gives away what he has and shares with others.

—NEW GUINEA ELDER

MAY 18

Too much emphasis has been placed on getting ahead, and too little attention has been directed to what is right. Have we told our children and ourselves to trust in a Loving Father because he can take care of us? We have no reason to boast of our brains and authority. If we have them, they show. If we ever say to ourselves and our families, "Just get by," we have planted bad seed. Getting by is a form of laziness. We are not supposed to be lazy. Trying to take someone else for a fool is being one ourselves. So pay attention to what is right and good, and the Spirit will take care of the rest.

Look at me. I may be poor and needy, but I am the Chief of a nation.

—RED CLOUD, SIOUX

MAY 19

We think about where we are and what we ought to do. We do this every day and what we decide puts our feet either on the right path or the wrong one. We know which is which, but we want to ask how much we can waver—if we step off of the right path just this once, can we get by with it? If we are tempted to do the wrong thing just this one last time, forget it. If we let it happen, it will ride us from now on. We never really forget anything that we know is wrong.

Right now is the time to be intelligent and not do something dumb. Turn away from wrong and go the other way. Move decisively. Act with the future in mind. If we make the right moves, we set in motion something we will always be grateful to have—freedom from guilt and freedom to be who we really are, free people with unlimited opportunities.

We had no teachers…we had no schools…we had to turn and look at Creation.

—MUSKOGEE

He that scatters thorns will sooner or later have to go barefoot. An intentional hurt is never forgotten. Life records it somewhere—the most beautiful place may hide the sharpest thorn. Go back and gather up the thorns you've scattered while there is still time. Not one sly plot, no matter how clever, can cover a wrong. Delusion is a boomerang that returns to its starting point with precision, and we cannot afford to stand there waiting. Look out for others, dilute bitterness, and have no part of envy. These "thorns" are merciless and have the potential to cause great pain. Avoid them at all costs. Instead, cultivate gentleness, which has amazing strength. It sweeps the path where people walk and it leads them away from dangerous places.

Wolf, I have considered myself, but the owls are hooting and the night I fear.

—GRAY HAWK, SIOUX

MAY 21

Everyone has the right to live what they believe, but all of us bear the consequences as well. Every day we have to deal with what we believed yesterday. When we wonder what we did to deserve something, we know we had something to do with what has happened, even if we did not plan for it. Each person has a personal belief of his own. It is his right to exercise it, even if it brings unhappiness and hardship. But try to believe and say things that bring about good. Listen to inner wisdom, hear the voice of the Spirit, and use it to improve circumstances.

I shall die before my heart is soft, or I have spoken anything unworthy of myself.

—CANNONCHET, NARRAGANSETT

Many people do good works, have good hearts, and find satisfaction in being busy, but it does not mean they never have problems or questions with few answers. Can anyone be so perfect that they live in ideal circumstances? No one lives who has not had their senses baffled and their faith challenged. But those who overcome these challenges have learned to step over, look past, and ignore all the reasons they should give up on life. Instead they embrace life and keep on living.

The Indians were religious from the first moments of life.

—OHIYESA, DAKOTA

MAY 23

Some words can be said any number of times and still be new. The Cherokee say, "*Gv ge yu a*"—I like you or I love you. I love you to the ultimate amount for one day. But it will not compare with tomorrow. Tomorrow brings its own container to be filled. As the sun rises and sets, time moves swiftly, and the need to be loved never changes. It helps us appreciate the finer things, knowing our hours together are as beautiful as polished gems that never lose their glow and always retain their value.

Silence, love, reverence—this is the trinity of first lessons.

—CHARLES ALEXANDER EASTMAN, SIOUX

MAY 24

A nest of baby birds under the eaves produces joyous peeping each time the food arrives. Even though they are out of sight, it is not hard to imagine their mouths popping open at the sound of their mother's approaching wings.

Scenes like this are not unusual on a spring day—warm sun, soft breezes. And an abundance of food that comes from some source we do not comprehend but from which we receive freely anyway. Spirit is generous. Are we thankful?

We speak from our hearts, and memory records our words in the hearts of our people.

—GRIZZLY BEAR, MENOMINEE

MAY 25

Spring storms are coming through, with wind that twists the trees until their limbs break. Thunder crashes and lightning flashes. It is hard to resent all the fireworks when moisture is needed, though the loud storm results in little rain—just like a ruckus among humans. Good gentle rain without all the fuss is not easy to come by, but it does happen and then everything benefits.

Like gentle rain, diplomatic work among labor and government and corporations is so important. If something can be settled with gentleness and firm determination, why not? Unfortunately, some people will not listen without the fireworks. Because of this, peace and harmony must be spoken before negotiating begins. They are hard to remember in the heat of things; it is hard to hold in line when someone is angry. Yet peace and harmony are crucial. We must work hard to make them a part of every negotiation.

You can usually learn what you need to know by watching and listening.

—NATIVE ELDER

Never talk about your troubles. Never look for sympathy, because the need to commiserate only causes more misery. Resist the urge to exaggerate difficulty, because that will only result in a bigger mess. Some claim if you talk about it, it relieves the misery, but don't believe it. If a seed of misery is planted, it will grow like a weed in spring. Talk sickness, lack of money, companionship, or freedom, and that's what you will get—until you weed out and destroy that talk of misery. Negative talk is a bear trap set in a hidden place and it snaps at whatever comes near. The pain is unbearable, so put it away from you. Instead, talk about sufficiency and every good thing, and they will be yours.

The Great Spirit will not punish us for what we do not know.

—CHIEF RED JACKET, SENECA

MAY 27

Anyone who has ever woven a basket, made a quilt, or painted a picture knows the importance of mixing colors and textures. One or two things may not make a picture, but overall the distinct pattern of life is laid out for everyone to see. We may be aware of how we weave our lives on a daily basis. Weak strands, colorless fibers, and questionable design shows more than we know. What seems bright and perfect and trendy may make an overall picture lacking life. Sometimes the drab and unattractive pieces bring out the cheerful. Every part of who we are has given us the power and strength to do wonderful things. Rather than glancing backward to see what we did wrong, look ahead. Choose gratitude and unjaded joy in all the little things life weaves together so brightly.

Had the Indian been as completely subdued in the spirit as he was in his body he would have perished with the century of his subjection.

—CHIEF LUTHER STANDING BEAR, LAKOTA

We can be overwhelmed by what we have done and what we failed to do. Learning to forgive others is a cinch in comparison to forgiving ourselves. Someone once said that God is like a mother who can kiss away to oblivion anything we do wrong. We need to remember that.

Only time heals some wounds. We can't go on irritating old hurts and expect them to heal. Yes, we have all done wrong things, but we cannot let them whip us. We can forgive and we can be forgiven.

I am a poor man, but I am not going to get angry and talk about it.

—SATANTA, KIOWA

MAY 29

A voice in our ear pleads for us to pay attention. Listen closely, see with the eyes of the mind, because so much will pass us by if we are asleep. No need to go blank in our minds, no need to stay motionless. Go on with good work and keep the mind open to ideas and to the brightness of each new day. Many beautiful things wait to be discovered if we will only open to them.

Our minds are like lush green fields, but we too often plant weeds there by taking in inane stories and dwelling on all the wrong things. Stop listening to rumors and hearsay that may or may not be true. Cultivate the highest and the best—and be the best!

God raised me with one thing only.

—CHIEF GALL, HUNKPAPA SIOUX

Before we ever get to know people, their experiences have influenced them with certain ideas and formed their personalities so that we may not be able to blend with them. We all have past experiences that set us firmly in our own ways. We should consider these things before agreeing to join forces with a person we may not truly know. We like to think we can fix anything with enough love. But love means being honest, especially about personality differences that may lead to hostility if we force ourselves to work with someone with whom we are not compatible. We cannot change others. We can only change ourselves, but that may not be what is needed.

We are good and not bad.

—RED CLOUD, SIOUX

Some people know how to give unreservedly—not once or twice but over and over again. They never consider whether someone is deserving or not. A friend is a friend. It is enough. How good it is when one person goes out of the way to bless another—for no particular purpose other than to make someone happy. Sometimes such effort is shunned or ignored or thought unimportant, but love cannot be overlooked that easily. Without love, what would the world be? We need to say thank you to these special people in our lives. When someone refuses to see our faults and continues to love us and be a friend, how can we be anything but blessed?

You and your brothers press on, let nothing discourage you.

—TEEDYUSCUNG, DELAWARE

JUNE

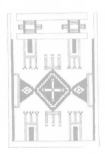

GREEN CORN MONTH

DA TSA LU'NEE

JUNE 1

A real champion started "back there" with the right intentions, the right stuff, the full ability to be a champion. Many of us would like to be champions, but our knowledge is so limited and we are often selfish. We need help. Be unpretentious when you ask for help. If you do not have wisdom, ask for it—but don't rely on another person to meet all your needs. Sometimes those we depend on, those we choose to mentor us, have feet of clay. But when people disappoint us and we encounter obstacles in our path, we must continue to work toward our goal. This how a champion is born.

If we have corn and meat and know of a family that has none, we divide with them.

—BLACK HAWK, SAUK

JUNE 2

All our experiences refine us—and sometimes they try us to the bone. But when we've made it through a trying experience, we know that the next time we face this thing we will know what to do.

The old way of breaking and training a horse was to get on it and ride until it quit trying to throw the rider. Thank goodness, there are new ways now to gentle a horse, but many of us act like a horse being broken the old way. We buck and snort until we throw the rider, and even then we're still wild and poorly adjusted. Most of us don't like being refined. We want to do it our way—and we pay the consequences for that. It's important, though, to remember how strong we are when we learn—and how weak when we react. Our challenge is to be open to learning throughout our lives, knowing that what we learn will help us with whatever we encounter in the future.

Press on with all your might in promoting the good work we are engaged in.

—TEEDYUSCUNG, DELAWARE

JUNE 3

In a time when so much seems to be gained through intimidation, gentleness still has amazing strength. Gentle friendliness can make everyone feel they are part of an important team—a team that is based on respect, confidence, and a willingness to help. When we lose the gentle touch, we lose control. Little else counts after our limits have been exposed. Little counts when our self-respect is gone. When we resort to hard talk, we may think we show our superior ability. Instead we show a weakness of character. The need to put someone down in hope of looking good only reveals a real lack of gentility.

It has never been wise to underestimate the person who has gentleness, compassion, and understanding. These qualities endure and help build a better world.

Our minds are agreed.

—CHIEF RED JACKET, SENECA

JUNE 4

Some people abandon ship when the seas of life get rough. When it gets too hot, others back away from the fire they built to roast someone else. We have seen weakness, panic, and hurt in people, but we have also seen strength and purpose where we least expected it to be. The weakest person alive can be touched with something golden, something that comes from some deep inner place.

We cannot know why these things are so, for only spirit discerns. Only in spirit can we know what is truth and what is devised to fool the eye and heart. It is spirit that teaches wisdom about these things. We need only ask.

Father, be strong and take pity on us, your children.

—PONTIAC, OTTAWA

JUNE 5

Except after a rain, the summer creek flows slow and easy. A low-hanging tree floats its leaves in the water and a good-sized crawdad piles up a circle of mud as he digs a hole in the wet bank. Little eddies twirl inside the arm of a dead limb lying at the water's edge, and water bugs skate where the water is calm. This is where Grandpa used to call the owls—he was so good at it they didn't know he wasn't another owl. Here a copperhead bit my cousin, and here we fished hour upon hour, catching nothing but sun perch. A flood washed in an old wooden boat, flat bottomed and without oars. But we knew how to make do, and the old boat sparked our imaginations as we created wonderful adventures. Going to the creek may not have produced anything tangible, but the peace of mind and relaxation we experienced there were invaluable.

Six years ago I had the pleasure of making peace with you.

—CORNPLANTER, SENECA

JUNE 6

Nothing can humble like hearing E lis i, grand-mother, say, "Remember, pretty is as pretty does." It takes an older person to see the foolishness of pride. Nothing good comes of it, and there's the continual pressure of having to keep it up. Pride never allows us to relax and be ourselves. Instead, it strains us beyond the breaking point.

Someone said that the small have a pride that is infinitely great. But pride can be brought down to earth by memories of very meager beginnings and a good dose of humor. We can be glad, we can be forever grateful, but we need always remember that pride walks pretty and falls flat.

Is it wrong for me to love my own?

—SITTING BULL, SIOUX

JUNE 7

Too often we allow our emotions and feelings to dictate our lives, but emotions are not always dependable. We too easily connect the present moment with all the other times we have been hurt and the result becomes overpowering. Sometimes we discover too late that what we thought and believed in a tense moment was not true. So how do we deal with emotions? We can center ourselves in a faith that does not waver in the face of emotion. Our faith will support and guide us when we are incapable of seeing with a clear and unprejudiced eye.

We do not wish to destroy your religion, or take it from you. We only want to enjoy our own.

—CHIEF RED JACKET, SENECA

JUNE 8

We prolong problems and severe personal upsets by repeatedly going over them in our minds. Our minds are like a movie screen on which we project images hour after hour. When we change these images from bad ones to good ones, we will quickly recover from our problems and upsets. Once we see the folly of constantly watching destructive images, it's easy to let go of them. What once seemed like loss, now becomes a gain. We become healthier and stronger when we focus our minds on positive images. The most successful survivors of the Depression years took great pleasure in seeing potential gain where everyone else saw loss.

The Great Spirit Chief will smile on this land and wash out the bloody spots from the face of the world.

—CHIEF JOSEPH, NEZ PERCE

JUNE 9

It is strange how something can be so important at one moment and totally unimportant at another, with a very short time in between. As we grow, our spirits grow and we let go of ideas, attitudes, beliefs, and feelings we once thought were set in concrete. As lovely or unlovely as something may be, it never stays the same. It cannot. It grows into something newer and richer, or it gives way to nothing.

Life is a fluid thing, and we need to "go with the flow." If we become rigid and inflexible, we can too easily be shattered. We need to be softened by love. Love is the spiritual force that girds us in our weak moments, heals us when nothing else can help, and gives us purpose. Love not only gives us life, but it also helps us to live life fully and with contentment.

I thank God that I have this opportunity.

—CORNPLANTER, SENECA

JUNE 10

We receive a special kind of education when we focus on and observe our thoughts. Where does our train of thought take us? Does it take us nowhere? Does it take us to old places where we relive pain and bad experiences? Does it take us to exciting new destinations? Often we are not aware of where our train of thought literally takes us. We need to choose our "train" carefully so we can go to good destinations instead of destinations that defeat and discourage us. At its best, thinking is the soul talking with itself. Ask yourself, "What does my soul say today that I should heed?"

The world is a library.

—CHIEF LUTHER STANDING BEAR, LAKOTA

JUNE 11

Success or *a s qua dv*, as the Cherokee says, is a sense of doing something well and reaping the accompanying rewards. We need to take care, though, that a little success does not lessen our efforts to do something well. We must persist for however long it takes and give whatever is required of us. We have to keep stretching our limits, refining our spirits, and renewing our minds.

For the Cherokee, home, land, and family are most important. But success means different things to different people. Dignity and respect, however, are prerequisites for success. To succeed, we also need a spiritual foundation that is not based on buildings and people, but the inner power and strength of the individual.

I want this peace to be legal and good.

—GERONIMO, APACHE

JUNE 12

Would you save our souls by educating us, showing us how to worship, instructing us in what clothing to wear? Who is the Indian that has survived in a healthy atmosphere for all these centuries?

Several of our young people were brought up in your colleges. They were instructed in all your sciences; but when they came back to us they were bad runners, ignorant of every means of living in the woods, unable to bear cold and hunger. They didn't know how to build a cabin, take a deer, or kill a deer. They were unfit hunters and good for nothing.

—CANASSATEGO, LANCASTER

JUNE 13

The need for perfection makes us say, "Standardize, make it all the same thing"—but do we think the same? No. How can we standardize and all be alike? The way you are is perfect for me. I have no desire to change you. All the change that I pray for is that you be happier, that you see how life is a journey, not just a destination. See it all minute by minute, hour by hour. I pray that you take no time to complain or weep for what might have been. Make this moment one to remember for its joy and for all the blessings that have come upon you. Time is dear and complaining wastes time. Rise up and rejoice!

I was not brought here from a foreign country.... I was put here by the Creator.

—MENINOCK, YAKIMA

JUNE 14

Is something you thought you were rid of trying to come back on you? Refuse it. If it did not work before, it's not going to work now. If it is an illness, see yourself as whole. Tell the illness to be gone. Stir yourself up and feed such powerful thoughts to spirit that the devil himself cannot control you. Decide what you want and go after it. Speak to the mountain and speak to the valley of the shadow. It is your right to do so. Even a few hours of taking charge will make all the difference. Try it and prove to yourself what a powerhouse you are.

I am a man, and you are another.

—BLACK HAWK, SAUK

JUNE 15

On occasion two people will get the same idea, but it is the one with persistence and determination who brings that idea into being. That person didn't let the idea escape, but spent time with it, seeing and tasting its possibilities.

How many of us have been surprised by someone else having the same idea or thought we did? We dallied with it, spent time wondering if it was worthwhile, and wasted the power by talking about it too soon. In the meantime, the other person thought about it and set right to work perfecting every detail.

Life is not going to wait on those who dally. We have to learn where the start button is and lose no time hitting it.

We are like birds with a broken wing.

—PLENTY-COUPS, CROW

J U N E 1 6

What is so rare as a day in June? An Indian who has forgotten to worship, who does not meditate on his heritage, who eats all the wrong things, and who forgets to breathe deeply of God's green earth. We are not to blame for everything, but we do know we learn as we go. The Great Spirit leads us where we should be if we listen— and we do listen because it is life to us and health to our bones.

Legends are related about the contempt and disgrace falling upon the ungenerous and mean person.

—OHIYESA, DAKOTA

JUNE 17

M ost of us would be slow to answer if we were suddenly asked, "What is your deepest desire right now?" Even if we have a vague idea about what we want, we probably would not have a clear-cut picture in our minds. A whole series of questions would probably run through our minds: What could possibly happen that would fulfill my desires? Am I afraid to answer because I might miss out on something bigger?

Why is it that we possess many material "things," but don't know our own heart's desire? Not knowing our heart's desire explains why we sometimes pray and our prayer goes nowhere. It goes nowhere because we cannot be specific. We fumble and change our minds and though we work hard, we accomplish nothing. But when a dream—a heart's desire—is shaped and colored and surrounded with joy, it happens. It happens when we know exactly what we want.

The answer you brought us is not according to what we expected.

—JOSEPH BRANT, MOHAWK

181

JUNE 18

It's comforting sometimes to hear the cicadas and locusts buzzing in the trees. Early in the season they only sang in the evening, but as the days grew warmer they began to fill the woods with their primitive sounds all day long. Sounds of nature have a perfect rhythm that slows our own frenetic pace and gives us rest. Just sitting outside for a few minutes can change a whole outlook. Don't have time to sit outside? You must make the time—it is worth all the effort, and the blessing is so great it lasts into the days that follow.

The earth is the mother of all people and all people should have equal right upon it.

—CHIEF JOSEPH, NEZ PERCE

JUNE 19

Saying what could go wrong sets the biggest spring on the meanest trap we could ever imagine. This kind of talk is subtle and dangerous because what we say goes into our subconscious and triggers future events. Talk is creative—it builds spaces in which to store what we talk about. Even if we occasionally say positive things, our minds cannot get to them because they are blocked by all the negative things we've said.

Do no throw words on the ground. They should be kept by us. It is to our good that we keep our words on a high level.

—LITTLE RAVEN, ARAPAHO

JUNE 20

One day the vegetable garden looked pitifully dry and the vegetables just weren't growing. Then a surprise summer shower pushed through. The very next day the pepper plants and tomatoes started to bloom and "set on," as a good gardener knows will happen. Give life a chance. Don't plow under hopes and dreams before a surprise shower comes through to replenish them. Even if showers aren't predicted, know that this is "due season" for many things due us. Be a positive prodder and predict what you would have happen. We have not because we ask not. We must collect what is owed us by making a simple request and then giving thanks that we have not been forgotten.

We have told you our patience is worn out.

—JOSEPH BRANT, MOHAWK

JUNE 21

Doubts? Sure, we all have them—doubts born of past circumstances that make us believe there isn't a chance. But when we were born, we were equipped with a full measure of faith. No one, absolutely no one, received more than we did. It is just that we have a hard time believing we have such faith, so we opened up and let doubt come in. Now we need to open up and let all those doubts out—insist that they go. We cannot harbor them because they are rooted in fear. Fear is an emotion—and emotions can be managed by faith. Claim the full measure of faith that you were given at birth, and let those doubts go.

You have told us to speak our minds freely, and now we will.

—LITTLE TURTLE, MIAMI

JUNE 22

Breezes whisper morning *suna-lee* songs through lush oaks and up toward the feathery groves of willow. Red-winged blackbirds search the reeds for nesting places and trill about their territory. Life, in its ebb and flow, moves in these woods with the precision of the Breath-Maker. Dappled patterns shift and color the mossy paths with a sweet cleanness to touch the soul of anyone who tarries. Wild sweet william and honeysuckle scent the air currents, and there can be no doubt—it is June! So much must be absorbed in a short time because the next act is waiting. Raccoons eye the apple trees, and jays chortle in the cherries. Nothing is new here, but everything old is new again, including the casual observer.

He finds all his needs in the pleasure of hunting and fishing.

—MICMAC CHIEF

JUNE 23

Acknowledging joy works like yeast in bread dough. When yeast is activated by kneading it into the other ingredients and kept warm and handled carefully, it expands into lovely loaves that brown in the oven and gives off an unbelievably wonderful fragrance. We have to help the good things grow into such strength they cannot be challenged by recalling anything of unhappiness. Unhappiness has visited all of us—and all of us have to decide when it should leave. Don't cherish the bad times but smother them out of existence with the good. It works.

Love one another and do not strive for another's undoing. Even as you desire good treatment, so render it.

—HANDSOME LAKE, SENECA

JUNE 24

Most of us think of "grace" as something lithe and flowing and without rough edges. Actually, grace is a blessing that comes without having done anything to earn it—a free gift. Henry Ward Beecher said that God equips us with grace in order that we may be nurses to other people's weaknesses. Instead of nursing someone's weakness, why not help them find grace? More people have the gift of grace than realize it. Too often, they smother it with selfishness and flaring tempers. We are all guilty of such things, but we can overcome them if we really want to be gracious.

Many older people are rich in grace because they have learned that it produces peace instead of tension. True grace simply knows the truth and lives by a creed that is the essence of gentleness, joy, and the willingness to help.

It is my wish and the wishes of my people.

—CORNPLANTER, SENECA

JUNE 25

Hay mowing has begun and golden bales dot the fields. Abundant rains have brought us yellow coneflowers and coreopsis across the prairies, and soon there will be many different kinds of sunflowers that love the heat of July. Not long ago we were told by those who know these things that we could expect drought, but the rains came. It seems to be a wait-and-see thing rather than a cut-and-dried fact, as it is with so many things, even in daily personal events.

When we hear negative predictions we can say, "...except for faith." If we believe it can be different, it can—even when we are tempted to believe the experts who make these predictions. But the Creator is even more able. We must not forget.

Mortal man has not the power to draw aside the veil of unborn time.

—POKAGON, POTAWATOMI

JUNE 26

Worry is a form of meditation—thinking and dwelling on wrong things. Worry is a negative tool used against us. It is a wrong force that needles us into submitting to possibilities we would not ordinarily accept. Henry Ward Beecher said worry is rust upon the blade. We are simply not as sharp when we worry.

If a child should chance to be restless, the mother raises her hand, "Hush! Hush!" she cautions tenderly. "The Spirits may be disturbed."

—OHIYESA, DAKOTA

J U N E   27

We can stand where we are or stand on tiptoe and look over the edge. What is the edge? It is that place where fear lurks and no one dares get too close. Many dreams have taken us up to the edge. With quaking knees, we have looked over the immense distance between what is and what could be. Most people turn away from the edge—it's just too scary. But we don't have to turn away. We can go to the edge and leap, if we can believe in something greater than can be explained. The most important thing is to let go of fear and take hold of the life whose Light never goes out.

The Indian reveled in being close to the Great Holiness.

—CHIEF LUTHER STANDING BEAR, LAKOTA

JUNE 28

Can we see the wind? Can we see the scent of pines? Can we see thought or what changes a tree's colors? We only see evidence. All the invisible that charms and sweetens life is just as real as what we can see. It makes us wonder why we question our own place in the plan of life.

Spirits are all about us—in a gust of wind, or a light
wind whirling around our door, that is a family spirit
of our loved ones, wanting to know that we are safe....

—GRANT TOWENDOLLY, WINTU

JUNE 29

What have we been thinking, what have we said, what have we resented? We get so wound up in all the things other people do and say that we lose our own perspective. When we find ourselves in such circumstances, we should remember the words of John Keats: "I cannot see what flowers are at my feet, nor what soft incense hangs from the boughs." We can't see anything good when we are so bound by resentment. Throw off all those weighty things and go free. Get rid of worry that does no good. We can stand up and go to meet freedom and it will come to meet us. No longer will we have to tolerate those overbearing moments in our lives.

Complaint is just toward friends who have failed their duty.

—TECUMSEH, SHAWNEE

JUNE 30

Late in the evening when the sun has almost set and activity begins to slow, it is so nice to sit in the garden to watch the birds taking their evening baths and to hear the night bird tuning up his evening song. It is almost mystical, as only a change of light can make it. Jet trails in the last rays of sunlight draw and redraw their lines in the sky. But way up there, they cannot catch the scent of petunias blooming down here.

Everyone deserves something beautiful to slow his or her pace at the end of the day. Don't count the things that were accomplished this day, don't regret, don't entertain thoughts that distress—just relax and touch the earth and see the sky. Let this be a time of gratitude.

May they always remember their relatives at the four quarters, and may they know that they are related to all that moves upon the universe....

—SLOW BUFFALO, LAKOTA

JULY

CORN IN TASSEL

TSA LU WA'NEE

JULY 1

The woods, rich from well-spaced rainfall, make almost solid shade so that nothing gets enough sunshine. The shade garden thrives from this unusual season and the hostas, caladiums, and elephant ears are in their glory. The ferns would like a little more light—which will come as the season advances. Light is so important to nature and to us humans. Seeing the sunshine on a hilltop or on a field of bright orange flowers gives us a spurt of energy because we are seeing life.

Sometimes when the sun is getting low in the west and seems unable to reach anything, an amazing event occurs: something begins to glow down in the dark woods. A shaft of sunlight has found an opening in the foliage and a tree glows as though from within. So it is with each of us. When we are inwardly lighted, we are greatly improved.

I don't want to settle. I love to roam over the prairies. There I feel free and happy, but when we settle down we grow pale and die.

—SATANTA, KIOWA

JULY 2

To be victorious we have to fall a few times. Though falling is not necessary to winning, most of us do it before we learn to avoid the things that make us fail. But when we begin to progress, even in little ways, we feel the flush of success and it urges us to make another try. As children, we fell many times before we learned to balance our legs to support us in whatever way we leaned. Nothing equals thinking big and doing big, but little victories lay the groundwork for winning to be so natural we don't even question that we can do it. Work first for the little wins, and then move to bigger things. Just a little honest success under our belts can make such a difference.

Give unto us that wisdom, which will guide us in the path of Truth.

—SOSE-HA-WA, SENECA

JULY 3

It often happens that our respect for an illness is more potent than respect for our own healing powers. We don't believe we can easily give up what brings us attention, even if that has placed us in difficulty. We certainly don't want something to be wrong, but the power of too much negative attention is subtle, mean, and seductive. Learn to fight fear and negativity. Nip the talk, the fear, the negativity in the bud right at the beginning before it has time to rule your life. Nobody wants trouble, no one willingly puts a hand to it, but it is easy to be fooled by the fearsome idea that nothing can be done. It can—but not by an outside force.

All things in this world have souls or spirits.

—EDWARD GOODBIRD, HADATSI

JULY 4

When recent storms totally destroyed several homes of lifelong country friends, their belongings were literally gone with the wind. Trees that took years and years to grow were stripped of leaf and limb. This tornado, with uncanny power, pulled a cement cover, wrenched the pump and pipe out of a large hand-dug well, but left a child's rocking horse sitting on the bare rafters of an upper story of what had been our friends' home.

Power and energy exist that we cannot comprehend. We humans can corrupt power when we can get a handle on it, but we have no conception of the power of nature until we see it. Suddenly we know there is something greater than us. Maybe we will learn that power is not greed—but spirit.

He was not a punishing God.

—CHIEF LUTHER STANDING BEAR, LAKOTA

JULY 5

Summertime meadows buzz with honeybees and the high hum of locusts—sounds of summer, slow as cold molasses and sweet and mellow as warm honey. Who of us doesn't have memories of many summers—running across hot dust with scorched toes, sitting on the porch, and talking about creepy things and scary incidents? Who does not remember the bright-colored zinnias and hollyhocks in Grandma's garden or fishing for sun perch in Big Creek and roasted corn on a handmade spit? Who has not walked in deep woods with foliage so dense that the owl called in the middle of the day? Who has not been caught in a rain shower and watched the huge drops splat on the broad leaf of the mayapple and felt it run in rivulets across one's face? Summertime is a well-traveled road of happy memories so that just recalling is a gift.

The most wonderful things a man can do are different from nature.

—TETON SIOUX

JULY 6

ook past anything that hides the limitless sky.
Look past buildings and wires and clouds to
where galaxies and planets and stars move and yet
hug their places in the plan of things. Look long and
hard at the second heaven and the third heaven.
What do you see? Nothing? So it seems, but your
spirit sees more than your eyes. The human spirit is
not as limited as some would have you think. Look
again, because there is nothing between you and
eternity. "Eternal" simply means endless, infinite,
lasting forever. We each stand in it at this moment.
What do you want to see? Whatever it is, keep your
view clear. Don't run toward the darkness if you
want to see the light. We too often crowd out our
ability to see far and clear with anger and frustration.
Free yourself to see what you want to see instead of
fearing every view as an enemy.

*The Indian loved to worship. From birth to death he
revered his surroundings.*

—CHIEF LUTHER STANDING BEAR, LAKOTA

JULY 7

We are often like children racing down a hill. The effortless speed puts us in danger of falling on our faces or running into a tree. Shifting down and slowing down take time, often longer than we think, and most of the time we need them sooner than we realize. What could be better in the summertime than having hours and hours in which to hear the songs of the cardinal and the meadowlark, to feel the sun warm and the breezes cool, to idle our engines by the humming of the honeybees in the locust blooms, and not have to think that in a few minutes this will end and then we'll be back to the old routine? We need time apart to renew, revive, and refuel. We need time to just sit and think. We need personal time to read and to rest our minds and bodies from the hectic and the hurried.

Continue unto us this goodness.

—SOSE-HA-WA, SENECA

Our habits make other people wealthy. As soon as they find out what we are reaching for, they provide it. If it is something good, we share their good fortune. If our habits lean toward the destructive, you can wager those who work to satisfy our appetites will keep working. Habit keeps us traveling the same routes, doing the same things, without thinking.

What would happen if we suddenly decided to change everything? Our habits would fight with us and make that change as hard as possible. Change is necessary in the way we think and in how we react, especially to the emotions that flare up when we try to let go of something destructive in our lives. When trying to get rid of bad habits, don't say, "I tried to do that before and it didn't work." We must not hesitate to defend ourselves against these negative forces. Everything depends on our being determined and persistent.

There was never a question of evil power over and above the power of Good.

—CHIEF LUTHER STANDING BEAR, LAKOTA

JULY 9

If you think you are so different you can never be like other people and share their lives, think again. Open the door to very special friendships. We need each other—we are needed by others and we need others. E li sti, my Cherokee mother, never separated herself from those who had needs, because she had needs as well. Her door was open, the porch was waiting for those who wanted to visit and share whatever was on their hearts. A lady named Sadie often came to visit, and we all loved her dearly. We miss her as we still miss our mother, and she loved us too. We may look different, we may be of different color, different attitudes, different wants and needs, but we are all human and share so many similar qualities that we could not miss knowing a friend.

Make the most of the other people, bless them, and give them friendship. It is a wonderful gift that is always welcome and always remembered.

What nation who has taken up arms ever brought peace and happiness to his people?

—HOPI

JULY 10

You know it is not necessary for you to approve of everyone. Some do not approve of you, and you are aware of it and pass it off—and so do they. It takes all kinds to make up the world, and those who do not know your nature or your intentions can judge with the same critical values you use. Your choice is to accept or reject. But condemnation doesn't help—not of others or yourself. If there's no balance in your mental, physical, and spiritual lives, then there is little power. But when the three parts are brought together in harmony, mountains are moved and changes are made. It is a matter of getting words and actions all in the right place to complete the picture.

Keep us from evil ways, that the sun may never hide his face from us.

—SOSE-HA-WA, SENECA

JULY 11

We don't have to see a wound to know it's there. We have all been hurt, sometimes beyond our ability to handle it. But this is the turning point, the hour of change: no more sinking down, no more fretting about what other people will think. This is a new hour, a new day, so run with it. Change things while you can. If you can't move the world for everyone, move it for yourself. It is in your control. Ask yourself, "If not now, when?" We tend to put important issues aside, ignoring our common sense and the strong message that it is time to change. Accept the challenge to change, because you may not have another chance.

Teach us to be like you, united.

—PAWNEE

JULY 12

When we do something wrong, we naturally tend to believe that there's no use in trying to rectify our wrong. After all, we have blown it, and we may as well go ahead and give it a full head of steam. Don't foolishly run into the fire; run from it.

As barefooted children, we often found ourselves in a bed of bullhead nettles, the most painful thorns. They grew close to the ground and spread out a soft green carpet that invited bare feet that had been in shoes all winter and were oh, so tender. Children learned quickly not to go any farther but to back out or call for help. The hurt may have been short-lived, but to keep on stepping where it was bound to hurt was pure stupidity. Adults can learn as quickly as children to stop and realize what going farther means. Learn to back out of painful situations and places of wrongdoing, and don't be afraid to call for help.

The moon leaves the sky to the glittering stars.

—E LI STI, CHEROKEE

JULY 13

Most of us fear that someone will challenge our right to be a certain way, to be able to do a certain thing. What will people think if they find out we are only ordinary human beings? What others think does not count for much. It is what we think about ourselves and what we tell ourselves that make all the difference.

Of course we are ordinary—why shouldn't we be? What is wrong with being a good person? Who can dare suggest there is something wrong with having high values and respect for ourselves? Think well of yourself, live your life well—and let others think what they want.

If we are wounded, we go to Mother Earth...to heal us.

—BEDAGI, WABANAKI

Change is upon us, and change always brings a certain amount of discomfort along with it. The very atmosphere of change is charged with things we don't quite understand. That makes us uneasy because we want to understand, we want to know. In short, we want to be in control.

When the winds of life are high and our situation seems unsettled, we begin to fret, not necessarily about the change but about how we feel. What we are feeling is a classic case of doubt. We're not in control and control is important to us. But the fact is that we are in control of the most important factor—the tongue. When a child or a pet feels distress, we comfort them with words, and we can do it for ourselves as well. Comfort yourself gently, and then face the change that comes with hope. The Spirit is with you.

We learned that Usen does not care for the petty quarrels of men.

—GERONIMO, APACHE

J U L Y   1 5

Walking up the summer lane late in the evening gave me a whole new perspective of the world. The hot sun was low on the western horizon and turning to see a sliver of new moon in the east, I saw the long shadows cast across the field. The dogs' shadows made them appear to be as big as horses. Human forms were stretched long and thin.

Suppose those late evening shadows were from our inner beings. Could it be that we are taller and thinner and more beautiful on the inside? Would it prove Mama right after all the times she tapped us on the back and told us to stand straight and walk tall? I hear her "huhm" in her Indian way. Seeing our own shadow is a surprise not unlike suddenly catching a reflection in a store window as we pass by: Who is that? A poor soul? Or a child of the King? Take your choice.

The earth says, it was from her man was made.

—YOUNG CHIEF, CAYUSE

JULY 16

You are capable of doing great things. Don't let anyone or anything convince you that you are weak and inept. Not true. You can do more than you think you can, and you can overcome all the barriers that have been raised against you. Never see yourself as unable to do any thing. Someone says that fat has overtaken them and there is no hope. Deny it. Tell yourself the truth—that you can do all things. And never promise yourself that "some day" you will have control. You have control right this minute.

Adjust your thinking, and above all change what you say to yourself. Words are so important, more important than anyone realizes. If you want to be free of excess weight or any other hangers-on, say you are free. Keep saying it. Say you are different from every other person, because you are distinctly different. Tell yourself you are not hungry, and soon your appetite will begin to adjust. You have the key to success right on your tongue. Use it.

We shall all be alike—brothers of one father and one mother, with the sky above us and one country around us.

—CHIEF JOSEPH, NEZ PERCE

JULY 17

How do we become wise? At one time we thought we knew it all, and later on we wished we had kept our mouths shut until we had learned something. When we hunger to learn, we discover that dipping into the depths of one thing is a way of tapping into the reservoir of all knowledge, because all of life is connected.

We begin to touch on wisdom when we see how much more there is to learn. Churchill said he was always ready to learn—he just didn't like being taught. So it is with most of us, yet we need to put our resistance aside and then listen and learn from life. Wisdom comes from observing and examining life not only with the intellect, but with the spirit. All wisdom comes from life itself, and from the One who created life.

I have heard that the earth is round like a ball, and so are the stars.

—BLACK ELK, OGLALA SIOUX

JULY 18

When we finally deal with a problem that we have tolerated for ages, we look back and wonder why it took us so long to resolve it. What kept us glued to circumstances that gave us no comfort or that left us furious at times? We may never know exactly what caused us to stay in a particular situation or to avoid dealing with a problem for a long time, but we do know what helps us finally resolve things: the Spirit. Something in us changes when we turn to a path that is spiritually healing and as perfect as a garden in full bloom. The sweet aroma of this good life, a life in which we've moved away from something destructive toward something good, is called freedom. With the help of the Spirit, we can live this life of freedom and unlimited dimensions.

The evil one came and demanded half the people. The Great Spirit said, "No! I love them all too much."

—KICKING BIRD, KIOWA

JULY 19

A car moving at normal speed down a country road in summertime sends clouds of dust beneath the trees and across the fields. We have not had much rain lately, and heat builds quickly along these dirt and gravel roads. Can anything survive the heat and dust? Yes! There along the fence stands the answer: great bunches of bright sunflowers.

Certain species thrive in dry weather and heat. Dust does not faze their beauty. If these beautiful clusters of bright yellow were people, many of them would ask, "Why doesn't someone do something about this drought?"

Yet other people don't question and complain. They learn how to survive like the sunflowers. They put down deep roots to drink from underground moisture; they stand against the winds and grow where they are least apt to be disturbed. They lift up their beautiful faces to the sun and they never murmur or complain.

We preferred our own way of living. All we wanted was peace and to be left alone.

—CRAZY HORSE, SIOUX

JULY 20

We often question why something happens to us, even though it's clear we've ignored the warning signs: stay clear of certain situations, avoid certain foods or drinks, avoid associating with certain people. We simply didn't use our common sense.

The artist doesn't paint sewage or trash but waits to paint something beautiful on the canvas. We are artists in our own way, deciding what we will paint on our canvas of life. When we don't discriminate, when we daub on and dip into ugly colors, we end up painting a picture that has to be done over. Often we paint with ugly colors simply because they were there or because other people were doing it. We are too lazy to paint something beautiful, or we're afraid our painting will be "different"—and we don't want to be different. Yet we need always to listen to the spirit within, which knows which colors to choose, what actions to take. When we do this, we will feel peace in our hearts.

There will never be peace between nations...until there is true peace in the souls of men.

—BLACK ELK, OGLALA SIOUX

JULY 21

An ordinary lizard about four or five inches long, with green and brown stripes along his shiny body, patrols the area around my window. He is diligent. He is industrious and can bend his body in many ways to get into crevices where bugs may be hiding.

Where there's a will, there's a way, as the saying goes. The lizard's will is his stomach. He can't afford to wait for legislation to give him food. He whole existence depends on making it happen by his own will and determination.

This lizard acts like a hunter, thinks like a hunter, and works to prove he is one. He looks for bugs more intently than most of us look for solutions for our problems. Both bugs and solutions float around us all the time, but we are wise to leave the bugs to the lizard and instead to focus on catching the solutions to our problems.

We live close to our great mother, the earth.

—SAGOYEHWATHA, SENECA

JULY 22

We are told that if we obey we will eat the good of the land. Can you imagine what that means? Everything for our benefit comes from the land: food, precious minerals, and every kind of plant that serves as medicine. Why would we want anything artificial when we can have the real thing? The Cherokee believes that just sitting on the earth or standing barefoot on it gives balance. The earth is not dead nor does it lack any good thing.

Obey and eat. Obey and be well. Obey and be happy. Obey and breathe easily and joyfully. Accept the gifts the earth offers. Obey and live!

Our God gives us...the corn and all things to sustain life.

—HOPI

JULY 23

Summer flowers have taken over the fields. Bright yellow cornflowers and coreopsis lay like beautiful blankets as far as the eye can see. Bee balm, fleabane, and Queen Anne's lace decorate as much space as nature allows. Create a garden for yourself—a garden of the spirit or a garden of the earth. Create a feast for the eyes and for the soul. See your garden as the miniature of life that the Spirit wants for you. You were never meant to be without beauty. Cultivate it wherever you can.

The man who preserves his selfhood ever calm and unshaken, his is the ideal attitude and conduct of life.

—OHIYESA, DAKOTA

JULY 24

A person doesn't take care of the past in one fell swoop. Making peace with oneself comes in stages, and very often when we least expect it. But we need to do it—even if it means going back and looking the devil in the eye. We need to know we are no longer under the influence of past experiences, especially negative ones.

Time slowly but surely removes the sharp, annoying stones that have been in our shoes for years. We know we still have miles to go when something still fills us with anger. But when we can look with curiosity and disinterest upon a bad experience from the past, we know we have turned a corner. This is a spiritual turning point. Celebrate it and give thanks to the Spirit who makes it possible.

No man can claim to know what is best for mankind.

—FOOLS CROW, LAKOTA

E merson said, "The louder he talked of his honor, the faster we counted our spoons." We hope no one wants to count their spoons after hearing something we say, but every person expresses himself differently. A feeling of inferiority makes all of us want to appear in the best light. If no one else says something kind about us, we may, out of the need to be equal with others, say something that irritates other honorable natures. And yet, here again, we could let it go by without comment. To be one's self is the best way to show our honor. If we care who we are and we try to be decent people without a need to compete, we are doing something honorable. Who we really are is always honorable—it is what we have erroneously added to it out of insecurity that rattles the spoons.

You say you are right and we are lost. How do you know this is true?

—CHIEF RED JACKET, SENECA

JULY 26

An old Indian chief once told the governor of Pennsylvania that Indians are not easily frightened. He said his people let the mice play in the woods without being afraid of the sound. Neither were they afraid of the sound of the wind in the woods.

How many times have we heard a bump in the night and went, with trembling knees, to locate the source? Things scare us when we least expect it. Maybe that happens in order to remind us to be alert—but not to live in a tense way. Let things happen, even check on them, but try not to run scared all the time.

When I was ten I looked at the sky and I knew there was some great power.

—SITTING BULL, SIOUX

JULY 27

The slightest gust of wind can ruffle the surface of the pond so that the reflection of everything around it is distorted. A troubled thought can do the same thing to our minds. We cannot control the wind, driven as it is by nature. But we can control our own minds, examine our thoughts, and decide what they are founded on and why they distress us. Many times we find that we have picked up on someone else's trouble. We want to help, but we need to resist making their problem our own. Help others, of course, but do not let yourself take on their burden as your own. The best way to help others is to learn how to handle our own walk of life so that we do not stumble. Then you will be strong enough to help and strong enough to be an example to others.

I bring you word from your fathers, the ghosts.

—KICKING BIRD, KIOWA

JULY 28

Mark Twain said that noise means nothing—when you hear a hen cackle you would swear she just laid an asteroid, and you know it was only an egg. Most of the time when we hear someone exploiting some great deed, you can figure they just laid an egg. When people do something really great, they don't have to insist on others taking notice. Others notice on their own.

Truth needs no shouting. It can whisper along as surely and quietly as deep running water. It has endured from the beginning of time. Isn't it a wonder, then, that when we discover truth for the first time, we call it miracle?

All of life is Spirit.

—LAFLESCHE, OSAGE

JULY 29

H enry David Thoreau was a man who loved simple things and the uncluttered life. He went for a time to live in the woods and made the best of life with meager things—and he loved it. Because he did not have to work away from his home, he had time to think—and he thought deeply. Few things escaped his scrutiny. Ralph Waldo Emerson liked Thoreau, but he wanted to teach him how to be Emerson, and it was not possible. Thoreau didn't even want to think and write like Emerson, so he chose to say what he said with simplicity. He said, "If you would convince a man that he does wrong, do right. Men believe what they see. Let them see." What could be simpler? And how easily forgotten. We believe, or tend to, that if people show wisdom, they must be trained to the teeth. No, it is more that they learn from their fellow human beings—and they keep the better part of what they've learned.

You all help me with supernatural power.

—YOKUTS

JULY 30

To a Cherokee, a moon is a time, a season. How long is a season? The time it takes to do anything, to produce a result, to do a job, or to spend a peaceful hour. A season is time, pure and simple. We seldom spend time doing what we love. Instead, we do what we feel is necessary—and many times it isn't necessary at all. Grandma Moses became a well-known artist at a ripe old age, but there was something very revealing about her comment concerning becoming an artist. She said, "If I didn't start painting, I would have raised chickens."

Most of us have a reserve of desires that will step in if we no longer do what we feel is necessary. What we are doing may be a vocation, but what we have reserved may be a peaceful thought. Were it not for my neighbors—the raccoons, possums, coyotes, and bobcats—I, too, would raise chickens. They are so peaceful.

By the same Great Spirit Chief they are all spirits.

—CHIEF JOSEPH, NEZ PERCE

Sometime, someday, I will know how to take living in my stride. I will know how to side-step a great many things, and completely ignore that many more. Someday I will learn to pay less attention to the unimportant and stop fussing about things I had nothing to do with in the past and cannot significantly change in the future. One day I will have finally gotten rid of all those things I saved for some reason, and then I will have room for what I really like today. As soon as possible, I am going to be less serious about some of the trouble I hear about. Soon I am going to sit in the sun all day and just be happy that I now have time to sit in the sun and be happy!

Everything is sacred.

—BLACK ELK, OGLALA SIOUX

AUGUST

END OF FRUIT MONTH

GALO'NEE

AUGUST 1

Powerful summer storms, filled with intense energy, send jagged lightning strikes across the sky accompanied by rolling, cracking thunder. Pressure changes, colors move from deep purple to white and greenish-yellow. When a storm threatens, most take cover. Earth is in continual change, using its natural power to destroy and renew, to dismantle and to make beautiful. And so it is with supposedly kind-hearted, civilized, and benevolent human beings. What often seems to be our right turns into a storm that devastates and throws us into the whirling eye of the storm. We are hurt and we hurt others, not because we want to but because we are trying to get around obstacles to a better place. If we can only be still, stop arguing, stop being offended, the storm will settle and life will move on.

For me there was always a sense of contentment.

—MAORI

AUGUST 2

There are right things to say and right ways of saying them, but we don't always say the right thing the right way. We have all been guilty of speaking without thinking. We have been guilty of talking when we should have been listening with the heart. A casual remark that may not mean much to us can strike a nerve with someone else. Sometimes we disregard the feelings of others by saying they are just too sensitive, but that does not justify our being callous.

Sometimes the tables are turned, and we would rather not hear what the world has to say to us. The chatter and clang of harsh words disrupts our nervous systems and hurts our feelings. This should show us that absolute silence is a rare gift, and we can help create it. We can think about what we are going to say before we say it—and we can refuse to be offended when someone else slips and speaks without thinking.

Sometimes we prayed in silence . . . at other times one would rise and speak of our duties toward each other.

—GERONIMO, APACHE

AUGUST 3

We yearn for loyalty, but we cannot demand it. Others must offer their loyalty to us—and we must earn that loyalty through kindness and decency. We must also wisely respect the basic rights of others, including the right of others to have their own opinions. Remember that one person's rights end where another person's rights begin. Mutual respect inspires loyalty: we must be loyal to those we expect to be loyal to us.

When this pipe touches your lips may it act as a blessing upon my tribe.

—BLACK THUNDER, FOX

A Cherokee elder once commented that it was not the things of the world that gave him peace but the rustle of sycamore leaves, smoke from a campfire, and an owl in the nighttime. As he leaned back in perfect peace, he sang in his native tongue about the "little people" who kept him company. The "little people" may come from Cherokee folklore, but we all have little people in our minds to keep us company. For most, these "little people" are created by thought, memory, and a touch of whimsy. Whatever comforts us in our minds and helps us avoid worry and fear, opens our deeper being to peace. We dare not entertain thoughts of malice but only sweet thought, so that sometime we may entertain angels unaware.

I have seen that in any great undertaking it is not enough for a man to depend simply upon himself.

—LONE MAN (ISNA-LA-WICA), TETON SIOUX

AUGUST 5

Emerson must have been speaking of this season of the year when he wrote, "The earth laughs in flowers." Delicate wild petunias—lilac in color—and white mallow have begun to bloom where it seemed nothing could grow. The heat of summer brings out sunflowers and pink verbena. Hay meadows have been cleared of grasses and bales, but wildflowers continue to bloom profusely. Black-eyed Susans fill the fields and purple ironweed nods its heavy head. Enjoy every flower because it was put here for a reason. Likewise, we were not put here by accident: we were put here to laugh with the earth. Please join the laughter!

What does it matter what I pray as long as my prayers are answered?

—SIOUX

Some people believe you can do something wrong to cause something good to happen. No way! How totally off course can we get in our thinking and acting? If we could move into the future and look back on what we're thinking today, could we believe it? What would our ancestors think of us if they could hear us talking about what is important and what isn't? What would old Indians think if they could see their descendants now? We tend to think that those who have gone before are gone forever, but that isn't true. Their spirits live, and ours will live as well. In all that we think and do, we need to remember that we are connected not only to the past but also to the future. All that we do, say, and think matters.

Everything on earth has a purpose, every disease an herb to cure it, and every person a mission.

—MOURNING DOVE, SALISH

AUGUST 7

We feel so alone at times. Even when others are with us, we look for that kindred spirit that may not have appeared yet. At other times we may be physically alone, but still have the deep knowledge that we are connecting with One more akin to us than a brother or sister. If we are wise, we will not always look to our own understanding. Instead, we will listen for the inner voice that tells us where to walk, when to turn right, and when to turn left. When we listen to the voice of the One within, we will know real peace.

From Wankan Tanka comes wisdom and power to heal.

—FLAT IRON, OGLALA

AUGUST 8

This morning, refreshing breezes blew up from the river bottom to cool shaded places where pockets of warm air were trapped. Summer subtly signals a change of season long before it actually happens. Something similar happens for us. We waver when we sense change, when we know the season of our lives is beginning to shift into something new, but we can't quite tell what it is. We detect something but have nothing to prove it. We can only wait and see what will come in the days ahead. The deer lifts its head to catch a scent of something different in the woods. Should it be afraid? We do the same—testing, sniffing the breezes that run hot and cool. We need this lull, this period of adjustment to study, to gather wisdom—and then move into the change.

It has come to me through the bushes...that you are not ready.

—BIG BEAR, CREE

It is better to be modest and earn a living than to be conceited and go hungry." This proverb points out how foolish it is to have such a high opinion of ourselves that we won't take an ordinary job in order to eat. Doing an honest day's work—no matter what that work might be—is as good as gold. Think of all those who carry bedpans, those who sweep, and those who wash dogs—how kind and considerate they are. It is a joy to know them. Giving service is a spiritual law that cannot be bent, broken, or hidden. It works. Commit yourself to this spiritual law and you will never go hungry.

Show respect for all men but grovel to none.

—TECUMSEH, SHAWNEE

AUGUST 10

British essayist William Hazlitt called silence in conversation a great art: communicating with one's presence, adding to the conversation without need of words. Comfortable little quiet spells in conversation are as rare as jewels. This is not so different from painting pictures. Often what we leave out is what makes a painting—or a conversation—outstanding.

Communication is so much more than just talking. Most of the time it is the silence that speaks eloquently. It allows everyone to take the responsibility for what is being said. But more than all the words we speak, and more than an exchange of information, silence gives us a chance to leave things unsaid. It is, indeed, a gift to ourselves.

Listen or your tongue will keep you deaf.

—NATIVE AMERICAN PROVERB

AUGUST 11

No matter how much we have learned or how much we know, someone else will always know a little more. That should never stop us from doing the best we can, because whatever someone else may know, we know something a little different. We have been created this way; we all have a purpose in life and we all have something to contribute to the world. We all need each other—and we need what the other knows.

Humankind has not woven the web of life. We are but one thread within it. Whatever we do to the web, we do to ourselves. All things are bound together. All things connect.

—CHIEF SEATTLE, SUQUAMISH

AUGUST 12

If you have tried to do better and everything has fallen apart, count yourself normal. If you feel you have taken two steps forward and slipped back two, that is normal too. This happens whenever we try to turn over a new leaf.

Something about making a change for the better stirs up negative forces. All the irritating things in the world will try to oppose you, but stand up to them and say, "Get behind me!" Then quickly stride out of the reach of those negative forces, and continue on your way toward the good. Soon your new leaf will flip over!

A man should train himself...to meet any emergency.

—OMAHA

When you are stressed, sit down and write yourself a letter, by hand. Then look at the words: Are they scrambled, the scribbling childlike? Are they angled up or running down the page? Steady your thoughts and very slowly begin to write again. Correct yourself as you go, no slanting back or leaning forward. There is a lot of you in that writing. If you study it you will begin to see what needs to be changed. Too many curlicues, too much abbreviation, too much scratching out? Recenter yourself to be yourself—in truth. Find that beautiful you and express the calm and energy-filled person that lies deep within you. You are you—and you are a strong foundation on which to build good things.

The life of a man is a circle from childhood to child-hood, and so it is in everything where power moves.

—BLACK ELK, OGLALA SIOUX

AUGUST 14

When you are very tired and nothing seems to be working, hold steady. This is the time when the tide turns and something speaks to your heart, even though it seems nothing has changed. Something moves near the surface of the mind and spirit just enough to lift the heart. It is not enough to make you shout, but it is enough to sit up straight. It begins so slowly that you think you just imagined it or that it was wishful thinking. No, don't let anything tell you it isn't real. Begin to give thanks, to rejoice in your heart. Begin to smile, even through tears. Begin to relax and breathe more easily. The change may not come in one big sweep, but it will come if you are expecting it. Weariness will ebb and hope will return—all because you dared to let it happen.

The Great Spirit is in all things.

—BIG THUNDER, ALGONQUIN

AUGUST 15

A real person exists beneath the surface of who we appear to be. We often hide our real selves to protect them from others who want to tell us how to run our lives. Sometimes we hide our real selves so long that we forget who we really are. Then we fall prey to many difficulties, especially those that come with trying to live our lives according to what others think we should do.

When we live our lives according to how others think we should live them, we cheat ourselves of our right and privilege to be ourselves. It may seem obvious (though it is often hard to do) that we need to be our real selves in order to act authentically and to make the decisions that are right for us. Issues that once confused us become clearer when we are aware of our own inner strengths, and when we no longer hide them.

We want none of your customs that we have not adopted ourselves.

—AHENAKEW, CREE

AUGUST 16

The tide turns—it always does. Nothing stays the same, nor should it. Living and thriving comes from taking every experience and turning it to an advantage. Situations that appear impossible make us believe we will never be the same. We won't be the same; we will be better. We will be better than we thought, because we say it. We will never be better than what we say. Saying makes it so. The law of life changes things. If we refuse to work with it, if we spend all our time worrying that we are going to be downgraded, we will. Be wise. Say what you want.

I am tired of talk that comes to nothing.

—CHIEF JOSEPH, NEZ PERCE

AUGUST 17

On dark nights when the moon leaves the sky to glittering stars and fireflies settle in close to the earth, E lis i, Cherokee grandmother, would say a change was coming. The power of her words sent messages deep into our hearts. Grandmother had said many things, and to us she had always been right. But these same summer nights gave us peace as well. Sitting quietly as currents of cool air moved around us, we heard the night bugs, locust, and katydids, sawing their tunes that lulled us into reverie. All these years later, E lis i comes back to remind us change is inevitable, and most of it because of what we set before us in word and act and deed. She also told us to meet our responsibilities, to sing and give praise for all our gifts, and never to leave a mess behind. She loved us, she loves us, she speaks the word.

Money cannot buy affection.

—MANGAS COLORADAS, APACHE

There is always something beautiful when we look for it—and always something wrong when we expect it. Even though experience takes us through territory we would not have chosen, we can always learn something. This is one of those times when rainfall is light and gardens need extra attention, but along the fences the sunflowers are perfect. They show us how to thrive when circumstances are not ideal. Straight and tall and exceedingly strong, these summer flowers prove they can take the heat.

Look for the beauty and expect things to take a turn for the better. They will—just as difficult times in the past have given way to better times. This time of trial, like others before it, will be forgotten.

As a present, anything we have you can take with you...but the land.

—CHIEF BLACKFOOT, CROW

When a person has lived a long time with trouble, it is not hard to recognize it from a great distance. Sometimes it is hidden behind a look of serenity, sometimes behind laughter— but frequently it is hidden behind jokes. When we really understand another person and know why he behaves a certain way, we also frequently sense that person's pain, even when he tries to cover it up. We desperately need each other to share our heavy loads and to know that, as different as we are, we are uniquely alike. It's important to remember that living is a two-way street: One day we lean on others when we need help, and the next day we give support to those who need us. We need each other.

He cures the sick by the laying on of hands.

—WINNEMUCCA, PAIUTE

AUGUST 20

Chief Luther Standing Bear said his Lakota people loved to worship. Contact with the Spirit was immediate and personal, and blessings flowed over them like rain showered from the sky. Can worship really produce such blessings? Indeed, yes. Indian people were born to believe this. To the Indian, Spirit is not aloof, not a figment of the imagination, but real life and real power. How sad that lukewarm attitudes silence those who do not want to be known as religious. It is not religion at all, but faith, Spirit, and something to rely on when life goes dry.

I was not lost. I knew where I was going all the time.

—SITTING BULL, SIOUX

AUGUST 21

Time and time again we feel the harshness of failing—even, or especially, when we bravely make another attempt to do something.

Most of the time we don't think about failure as an enemy, but it is. We simply have to plan a strategy that will carry us past that place where we once failed and help us to overcome all the things that dog our tracks—even ourselves. There are two necessary parts to this new strategy: first, strive to do better every day; and second, don't look back.

We always presume that the projects of our enemies are judiciously planned, and then we seriously plan to defeat them.

—PUSHMATAHA, CHOCTAW

Nothing equals the liveliness of a summer morning when the first rays of sunlight sweep a field of wheat ready for harvest. The honey-colored heads bow with the weight of grain and dew. Few of us could miss the peace that comes when the first light breaks through the foliage at the far side of the woods. It beams misty shafts of gold into areas untouched at any other time of day. It passes quickly and leaves the desire to see it again. And so the day begins.

No look of a lover could be sweeter than this deep trusting gaze.

—OHIYESA, DAKOTA

AUGUST 23

Make a point of learning what truth is, for it is what sets you free. Don't look for truth in all the traditional places, even though it may be there to some degree. You would never pick up bits of shells along a stream and try to fit them together by reason and logic. Reason and logic are of the mind, but truth is of the Spirit. If the spirit is not renewed, it seldom recognizes truth.

Other people cannot give us truth. They can only stir us up to find it for ourselves. We have to receive and perceive and believe—because the time comes when we have to walk by faith and not by sight. Life is really quite simple when we stop believing that money and fame are the essence of truth.

You can't wake a person who is pretending to be a-sleep.

—NAVAJO PROVERB

Our feelings have been known to betray us in the past. We cried when we didn't want to; we laughed in all the wrong places. We felt intense anger and fear and joy, always believing that nothing could change the way we feel. We believe we could never love more than we do—or hate worse. But every day brings a greater intensity, a new power to love more deeply and devotedly. And then we find new levels of disgust for what we cannot bear. One day we are stronger and more rested than another day. One day we can be angry enough to do what we would not consider at another time.

We learn to rely on our feelings, but our feelings leave us vulnerable and unprotected. We need more than feelings by which to live our lives. When we have principles, we no longer need to depend on how we feel. Instead, we can depend on what we believe. The Spirit will guide us.

The great sea has set me adrift, it moves me as a weed in a great river.

—IGLULIK

AUGUST 25

Thoreau told us that each person can interpret another's experience only by his own. For example, the pond reflects a day of blue skies, but when the sky is misty and gray, that too is reflected. The same pond reflects different conditions. So it is with us.

Trouble begins when we cannot understand our own experience—often because we don't want to. Instead, we focus on others. We watch how they behave, which may be totally different from anything we've ever experienced. Their actions and reactions may not personally apply to us, but we are in danger of believing they do. Instead of focusing on others, begin to study your own reflection, your own experiences. Understand yourself so you can then better understand others.

The sky blesses me, the earth blesses me. Up in the sky I cause the spirits to dance.

—CREE ROUND DANCE

AUGUST 26

We see certain things happen, and they enrich or drain us of all hope. How like the old Indian Chief Lone Wolf. He heard the night bird's clear song at the midnight hour, and he rose up from his deathbed totally well. The bird sang of good life and the old chief heard it. Listen for such a song in your own heart. You may experience your own miracle and rise like the phoenix out of the ashes of your life to become a new person. Life is filled with mysteries, like the recovery of Lone Wolf. Mysteries are often subtle and move quietly into our lives. Spirit does not shout to us, but what a wonderful thing when we hear Him whisper. Spirit's whisper is the very breath of life, the holiness of a moment of truth. Listen and hear it.

Sometimes dreams are wiser than waking.

—BLACK ELK, OGLALA SIOUX

AUGUST 27

The last few weeks of anything seem to take longer than all the time that has gone before. The last few weeks of summer are the hottest and driest, and it seems like forever before we get the rain we need. Not unlike waiting for the baby, we know it is going to be joyous but to the mother, those last few weeks are heavy and stressful.

Suddenly everything changes in a moment's time. It moves so quickly we can't quite grasp all the details. We have prepared, we think, and we are ready—we hope—but here it is and what do we do now? Being prepared is quite different from what we suppose. We have hoped and wished and prayed, but we stand totally awed until we have had time to digest it. The heavy little shower came in the heat of summer and was gone before we could listen and taste and record the details in our minds. Ready? Never quite ready—but willing to take it and be grateful as it comes.

Do the right thing and everything goes fine; do the wrong thing and everything is a mess.

—SPOTT, YUROK

AUGUST 28

There are many different kinds of success—and some are more important than others. There was once a wise farmer who was very successful in the planting and harvesting of his crops. But his success did not stop there. He not only cultivated his fields, he also cultivated his family ties. He believed his family was worthy of cultivation, and he reaped a rich harvest of love and respect. He was conscious that the required behavior was not born within him, so he cultivated the good, the true, and the beautiful. Was this gift his alone? No, the whole family—and yes, the whole world—grew richer and richer.

Why will you take by force what you may obtain by love?

—POWHATAN, ALGONQUIN

AUGUST 29

If you want to know why you are at odds with someone, think how people work from the brain. Some work from the left side of the brain, analytical and methodical, using reason and logic. Others work from the right side—creative and outside the limits of logic and reason. These two types may have no idea why their opposite sounds so unreasonable and even unreal. To the right side nothing is unreal. The invisible just waits to become visible. But to the left-sider the right-sider lacks strategy and order and consistency. He can't even lie straight in the bed.

We are different. Many things may fit together like a hand in glove, and twice that many may have to be thrashed out. But our willingness to see, our ability to give another person room to explain why his thoughts are different can avoid many a collision. Both need to have the wisdom to understand—and to forgive.

Too much of our thought only leads to trouble.

—IGLULIK

AUGUST 30

Don't complain. Complaining ages us. It also wastes time and gains nothing, not even honest sympathy. Begin to see the light—stop entertaining dark thoughts and worrying about unfairness and fear. Consider the fact that we have everything it takes to change our attitudes. If someone else is disagreeable, let them be, but don't react to it. We need to be true to ourselves and to the good nature of things and people and circumstances. Stop looking for things that are not right. Stop complaining, stop manipulating, stop saying "poor me."

Sleep no longer...in false security and delusive hopes.

—TECUMSEH, SHAWNEE

AUGUST 31

Remember, your words are the measuring cups that catch all the necessary things for good living. You can't say that something doesn't count, because every word is tallied on the positive or negative side. In this case, there is no such thing as balancing the negative with the positive—it must be all positive. Sometimes we want so much to say a certain thing that we do not control our tongues, and the bruising effect shows on our lives. We are puzzled about the cause of our trouble, but listen! Listen to your own complaints, your own disbelief. If was Dryden who told us that far more numerous was the herd of such, who think too little and talk too much.

We send our little Indian boys and girls to school, and when they come back talking English they come back swearing. There is no swear word in Indian languages.

—ZITKALA SA, YANKTON SIOUX

SEPTEMBER

NUT MONTH

DULU STINEE'

SEPTEMBER 1

If we aim at nothing, we can never miss. But it's important that we aim at something, so set a definite goal no matter how insignificant it appears to be. When that goal has been reached, set another. This brings success and starts a trend. Accomplishing something means progress that whets the appetite: do more and more, reach higher and higher.

Little steps cover great distances. Each one prepares us for bigger strides, and every idea acted upon produces another idea. Even though giant steps seem important, consider how the largest building goes up one brick at a time. The small careful steps—one brick, then another—give it strength and long life. Our confidence also comes in small packages, growing little by little.

We need to aim where it counts, but not so high that we lose sight of where we are going. And remember: take it one small step at a time.

Many proposals have been made for us to adopt your laws...religion...manners...customs. We should be better pleased to behold the good effect...in your practices.

—OLD TASSEL, CHEROKEE

SEPTEMBER 2

Who of us does not need to change, even though change scares the daylights out of us? We need change because it renews us and keeps us focused on giving the best we can. Yet, as much as we want to see something new and different, fear of it not being to our liking holds us back. But even if we hold back, nothing ever stays the same. Everything changes. Use it or lose it, as the saying goes.

There is no death. Only a change of worlds.

—CHIEF SEATTLE, SUQUAMISH

SEPTEMBER 3

E very person I meet today is going to have some special quality I cannot see. I must take it for granted that my eyes, as good as they are, are limited to what is tangible—to what anyone can see. What I need to know is that I also have inner eyes that can see beyond the boundaries of skin and bone to what lies within. Eyes do not have to be paranormal to see another's heart and soul. The inner eye is of the heart. See with the eyes of spirit and be wise to tender feelings and emotions.

I know the Great Spirit is looking down upon me from above, and will hear what I say.

—SITTING BULL, SIOUX

SEPTEMBER 4

Early morning fog hangs in a gauzy gray curtain all through the woods, and it can hang in the mind the same way. Even though it has no substance, fog obscures the very things that should be seen. Risk exists in blindness, not so much in physical blindness as in blindness of the heart. Those who are unable to see with their eyes are usually highly developed in other important areas that easily surpass normal vision. Colton put it aptly, "Men are born with two eyes, but only one tongue, in order that they may see twice as much as they say." A blind heart says too much and hears nothing. Ears that truly hear and eyes that truly see are very great blessings regardless of whether the hearing and seeing are physical or spiritual.

It is our desire that we be of one heart, having a mutual love and regard for each other.

—KANICKHUNGO, IROQUOIS

SEPTEMBER 5

A ny good thing you can say to me shall not be forgotten." These are the words of the great Comanche chief, Ten Bear. Ten Bear had been promised many things by Washington chiefs, but none of the promises had been fulfilled. He wanted to believe what he heard, but he knew in his heart that Washington wanted something he had, and they made great pledges to get it—with no intention of honoring those pledges.

A promise is serious business. It is a contract based on honor, whether it is written or verbal, and it cannot be held too highly. It is said that a politician thinks of the next election; a statesman, of the next generation. Ten Bear was a statesman, but men in Washington—sadly—were not.

We were the first here, us Aboriginals.

—AUSTRAILIAN ABORIGINES

SEPTEMBER 6

We imagine a bully as someone strong and huge and glowering. But bullies come in all sizes and use various kinds of intimidation: some manipulate, some use brute force, some use words. A bully is like a tornado spinning out of control—it respects nothing: self, others, or even animals.

Eleanor Roosevelt said we cannot be bullied without our consent. Is that correct? It is true that nothing feeds a bully like having someone resist, or try not to resist. But bullies can hurt us, and we need to remember that regardless of what someone says, we are worthy, we are intelligent, we are not to blame for what someone else is doing.

The earth and myself are of one mind.

—CHIEF JOSEPH, NEZ PERCE

SEPTEMBER 7

When the first misty rains of autumn begin to fall, we know that great change is upon us. Like all seasons, fall moves in and out several times before it settles down to the business of coloring leaves and laying flat the tall grasses. Subtle signs hint at what we know is inevitable. Overhead, flocks of migrating pelicans turn in lazy circles, loving the dampness that is their nature. All through the woods, Virginia creeper spirals up tree trunks in colors of flame. Each season has a quality of its own, and autumn is a meditation. John Keats called it "a season of mists and mellow fruitfulness." And when we can blend with it, we become mellow and fruitful as well.

> *The American Indian is of the soil, whether it be the region of the forests, plains, pueblos, or mesas. He fits into the landscape, for the land that fashioned the continent also fashioned the man for his surroundings. He once grew as naturally as the wild sunflowers; he belongs just as the buffalo belongs.*
>
> —CHIEF LUTHER STANDING BEAR, LAKOTA

SEPTEMBER 8

When everything seems too much, the struggle just to make it through the day is all consuming. Trying to have a good attitude seems ridiculous when the need to give up is so inviting. At a time like this, there are only two ways for us to go—one is up and the other is down. If we choose to do nothing, we slowly gravitate downward. But remember the alternative—up.

Choosing to struggle upward may not be a picnic, but overcoming something can be a great satisfaction. We just have to remember not to languish and fade, but to rise robust and determined. When we decide to do it, we will be able to do it—with spiritual help. Remember to say over and over that all things are possible for those who love the Creator.

The Indian's night promises to be dark.

—CHIEF SEATTLE, SUQUAMISH

SEPTEMBER 9

The earth is sacred to the *Tsalagi*, the Cherokee, as it should be to all people. Hardly anyone who walks the earth today realizes how important it is, or how it can produce when it is loved and cared for. Ordinary-appearing ground should be treated the way we want to be treated—with love and care. It should be cherished, not destroyed. When it is cherished and used wisely, it produces. Walk on the earth and sense with the soles of your feet the generations of life and blood that have gone into it. And when your heart races with fear, let this holy ground quiet you with peace and joy and patient endurance. Yield to the great loving power of the Breath-Giver, stand still, and rest.

[Arizona] is my land, my home, my father's land, to which I now ask to be allowed to return. I want to spend my last days there, and be buried among those mountains. If this could be, I might die in peace.

—GERONIMO, APACHE

SEPTEMBER 10

You are worthy even when it seems that you have failed and can't do anything right. You are worthy, and others will know it as well. Doing something wrong is enough punishment in itself without adding personal grief. Of course, you didn't do everything right; none of us does. But the fact that we have what it takes to get up and begin again speaks well of us. Billings said that if a man were perfect in this world, he would have to die immediately to enjoy himself. How true for those who cannot see the good in people who are less than perfect.

A single twig breaks, but the bundle of twigs is strong.

—TECUMSEH, SHAWNEE

We can't help but care what other people think. Something in our basic nature wants to please others, though some are never pleased no matter what we do. To live and work in harmony with each other means listening to other opinions—and reconsidering our own. Could we possibly be wrong about someone? Sagisaw in his native wisdom advised his brothers to wait—wait and see how long this opinion holds true.

Waiting to form opinions can at times be very wise. It is too easy to be negative, to say negative things about others, to accept the negative opinions of others. We need to weigh and sift opinions as to their importance—and their truth. Emerson said that the only sin we cannot forgive in each other is a difference of opinion. But maybe we need to listen more carefully, consider more wisely, forgive more easily, and censure less frequently.

Let me be a free man...free to obey every law or submit to the penalty.

—CHIEF JOSEPH, NEZ PERCE

SEPTEMBER 12

Walk straight and tall, and know there is no problem you cannot overcome. Find your footing and then stand up to challenges, insisting that the barriers give way. Sing when you want to cry, praise when you want to swear, and walk on with determination.

Challenges will always come—they are part of life—but don't make them your god. Never give worshipful attention to what challenges you. Know that the challenge is trying to take away your self-support, your dignity, and your will to overcome. Face it head on and insist that it be gone. Doing this is not easy, but with persistence and consistency, one day you will realize that you have overcome your challenge. Celebrate that victory—and know that you can overcome whatever new challenges may arise.

You are living in a new path.

—SITTING BULL, SIOUX

SEPTEMBER 13

The old self dies hard, and the new one must develop strength to face the challenges of life. Another way to say it is that the new self must develop sufficient "shock resistance." Give yourself time to become accustomed to this wholly new person. If you fail at first, so be it. Find the grace to rise above that failure and continue striving to live as a new person. So what if you need to start again several times? This is the way of life. You won't do everything perfectly the first time—no one does—but each time you courageously begin again, your new self becomes stronger. Don't put yourself down—or allow others to put you down. You are in charge: show the world your will and power to become your new self, your true self. Becoming and being a new and true self is your gift to the world.

When you find anything good in the white man's road, pick it up.

—SITTING BULL, SIOUX

In our time we have learned many things, and we have many more to learn. We have learned to walk and talk and rely on others—and to mistrust them as well. We have learned how to think, how to rate systems and people—and how to berate them. We form images in our minds, set up our value systems, decide how far we can go, and how little we have to do to reach our goals.

But somewhere along the way we decide we are not being shown the proper respect and we are offended. Do we have good reason to be offended, or is that lack of respect that others show us because our lives fall short in some way? It may be time to take another look at what we are doing—or not doing—with our lives. Is the world working against us, or are we working against ourselves? Our potential is great, but do we have the spirit to match it?

Argument doesn't pay; you don't come home happy.

—HOPI

Never ask anyone else who you are—only you can know your true identity. Only we can go into the secret places of our own hearts and spirits to map the outline of our personal lives. Things are stored in those places that no one else in the world could know but you. Do sit down with a notebook and write. Write what you feel so plainly that when you reread it, you will want to run. Don't hold back on the truth that underlies your most basic fear, your most earnest expectation. Tell the notebook what you want and what you expect. Laugh and cry with the words when they seem absurd. Stand up and shake off the darkness that is not part of you. Even if it takes a dozen notebooks, write until you know who you truly are. But don't let anyone else read your notebooks. Showing them to someone else— even those closest to you—depletes the power. This writing is mental and spiritual housecleaning. When you have done it, your spirit will be filled with more light and your heart will be lighter.

What I am, I am.

—SITTING BULL, SIOUX

SEPTEMBER 16

Feelings of rejection stem from worrying too much about what others say and think. Who cares what the curious and idle think? The truth is, those same people will quickly forget what they said and thought about you. You may hold someone's attention briefly, but too much is happening for any magpie to dwell too long on you—there are always more people to talk about. Relax. Keep calm and ignore the busybodies. This, too, shall pass.

With endless patience you shall carry out your duty.

—THE PEACE MAKER, IROQUOIS

SEPTEMBER 17

Develop your concentration. Cultivate the ability to focus on seeing through shadows that hide the truth. Never forget that things are not always what they seem. Some people may use tears, long faces, and sad stories to fool innocent others. Listen carefully and wisely—don't make judgments until you know what is true. Raise your consciousness to a new level and always look for truth. Remember that you are smarter than you give yourself credit for being, especially when you call the hand of a double-dealer.

A place where a man lives can shape his character.

—OLD KEYAM, CREE

SEPTEMBER 18

Walk away for a minute. Stop listening to bad reports. Stop thinking about pain and trouble. As concerned as you are, and should be, you are of no use to yourself or anyone else if you lose your strength of spirit. Rest. Mind, body, and spirit all need rest and a quiet place to restore balance. If the spirit is right, the mind tends to follow, and if the mind is at rest, the body relaxes more deeply. Remember always to think on these things: the good, the honest, the true, the beautiful.

We told them that supernatural powers...had given the Lakota buffalo for food and clothing.

—RED CLOUD, SIOUX

SEPTEMBER 19

Panic is the urge to run. It's not so different from a small stone tumbling down a steep hill: there's no stopping it. Panic is reaching for something, anything at all, because it might be our last chance. Or panic is rejecting something, because we are afraid of it or we don't want to do it. But what if this is something we are supposed to do and we don't know it?

Panic feeds on doubt and fear. But remember that spirit can free us from doubt and fear—and move us beyond them to a place of trust and love. When you feel panic, remember to pray: "Please, Lord, stop me if I should not do this thing. Please, Lord, guide me and give me strength, if I should do it." Then say to your heart, "Peace, be still." Calm the storm before moving ahead, because quiet serenity produces wisdom.

Under the tree of the Great Long Leaves, we spread thistle down as seats for you. Roots spread out from the Tree and these roots are called Great White roots of peace.

—THE PEACE MAKER, IROQUOIS

A miracle is something we don't have to explain. We don't have to explain where refreshing springs form or how the sparkling notes of birdsong come to be. We don't have to ask what causes the deep rippling laughter of a baby or what makes a shady lane so blissfully peaceful. Little miracles are endless: the healing of a memory, the disappearance of pain, a special spot of sunshine, or an answer to prayer.

Even we are miracles. We humans are a complex combination of experiences, attitudes, and gifts, and we always possess the capacity for greater things. More exists in us and for us than we can see or understand. That means the potential for more miracles is always present in our lives. We can take that potential and mold it, and remold it, to gain something eternal.

I am bringing something so the people will live.

—WHITE BUFFALO WOMAN, HIDATSA

SEPTEMBER 21

Darkness to a person in trouble holds only fear. The long night seems endless, but a bit of wisdom tells us that it is always darkest just before dawn. If that is true, and I think it is, the darkest hour means hope and a better time lie just ahead. With the passage of a little time, the light will edge in and fear will go.

When you face darkness, be strong and be of good courage—you are not alone. Spirit stands with you in the darkness and can transform you through the darkness. Many have experienced the way of darkness and have emerged far better persons, far stronger individuals. Darkness itself does not make anyone stronger. What makes you stronger is the shining of light on the spirit even when it senses only darkness. Trust that the light can overcome the darkness, and bring life and beauty to you.

Each step should be as a prayer.

—PLAINS INDIAN

How often it has been said that we cannot make it in this world without the proper background—often meaning that social standing makes or breaks the ambitious person. But only one background has been proven to be important: Were we kind? Were we thoughtful? Were we respectful?

Stop and think. If we respect ourselves, we have the proper background. If we respect others, it will show in what we say and do, and ultimately it will determine where we will succeed or fail. Good hearts—the best "background" anyone can have—never trample, never goad, never cause another person to fall. When we lift, we are lifted; when we respect, we are respected; and when we love, love abounds. What could be more important than that?

His face was very beautiful to see, and when he spoke my heart was glad and I forgot my hunger.

—KICKING BIRD, KIOWA

Things change. Life must change to exist and to endure. Anything rigid and set will eventually give way. Most people are opposed to change because they see no reason for it. But often we cannot control change. Then it helps if we change our way of thinking—one thing we can control—and lean more on the Almighty. Ask for wisdom, think without resentment, and show gratitude for every blessing and every favor. Be willing to do something different and do it with humility and determination. It will benefit you and show the world you can do anything.

If you have one hundred people living together, and if each one cares for the rest, there is One Mind.

—SHINING ARROWS, CROW

Nature, the expert gardener, shakes loose wisps of milkweed fluff to float across the meadows, always in anticipation of another season. But nature does this not in anticipation of the next season—winter—but for spring, when winter has come and gone. What wonderful long-range planning! Can we have such foresight?

The wisdom of nature tells us to plan ahead, to think about not only what will come tomorrow, but what will come—or be needed—in the tomorrows beyond tomorrow. Watch nature as it teaches us not to take things for granted, not to wait for perfection, not to lag when there is work to be done. Nature embraces life fully and works at what can be accomplished—though the results may not be seen for some time to come. Can we do the same? If we can, the work we do in our lives now will eventually bring spring meadows in full flower.

Cold days were the same to us as warm ones, and we were nearly always happy.

—PLENTY-COUPS, CROW

SEPTEMBER 25

At times we friends forget the road we've been down together, how difficult it was and yet how good. We grew up together spiritually, lending a bit of courage and giving a lot of love. Undoubted loyalty and understanding have been with us, and we have put aside anything we could not understand until it was clear. And we have been dedicated to each other, we've never excluded others or forgotten their importance in our lives.

God gave us each other to care for—to heap on love, to heal every rift, and to know we are never alone. We've planted good seed, and now it is time for the harvest, time to share what we have learned with those who have never known love and loyalty. This is the gift of friendship to the world.

Friendship between two persons depends upon the patience of one.

—NATIVE AMERICAN PROVERB

SEPTEMBER 26

Since soft autumn rains have fallen, the earth has taken on a new sheen of green, a restful, soft quietness. Yellows, bronzes, and russets begin to color the woods, and woodbine torches the treetops with brilliant reds and corals.

Across the valley the view is broadened to reveal blue-gray hills like elephant humps parading along the horizon. Smoke twirls up from brush cutting, and from a chimney or two, the first show of smoke from evening fires appears.

Fruit stands along side roads offer pumpkins in all sizes, a few melons, and squashes in countless colors and shapes. Harvest time, the season of abundance, is here. The busyness of the growing season now begins to slow. The gentle pace of autumn quiets us and helps us walk in serenity and peace.

Can you no longer dally?

—TECUMSEH, SHAWNEE

Notice how often your heritage kicks in to remind you of who you are. It may not make your hair any curlier or your eyes any shinier, but how the heart sings and lifts your spirits. At one time we knew how to be happy and glowing with health—we were glad just to exist. It was a glorious experience to run out on the basketball court and hear the people yell and the band play. We may never have made a goal, but this was sheer joy.

We didn't think of it at the time, but we were in the process of building memories. Now we do the same thing. Are these memories as good as the old ones? If not, make some that will be worth remembering. Forget the pain in your back and your fear of that pain. Recapture the ability to chew the sweet out of life—just the way we once chewed our bubble gum. Enjoy today so you can enjoy the memory of today—tomorrow.

Our lives are in the hands of the Great Spirit.

—TECUMSEH, SHAWNEE

SEPTEMBER 28

Last night coyotes congregated down the old road and opened their evening serenade with blood-curdling shrieks and shouts. The dogs were irate that such goings-on were taking place so close to their territory, but their barking did nothing to quiet the coyotes. It took my own shouts and floodlights to scatter the group of two or three, which sounded like a dozen.

That encounter with the coyotes offers a lesson to us. When negative rumors fill our territory, most people begin to cry and complain—like the dogs—but do nothing to stop them. But there is something we can do: Speak up—shout at those coyotes! Turn on the light of awareness to what is going on—and refuse to accept rumors. If we do not speak for ourselves, who will?

We are a just people.

—PUSHMATAHA, CHOCTAW

SEPTEMBER 29

Mother Nature is at it again. She says, *I have bedded down my things beneath a blanket of leaves and sometime later it will snow. I go to the trunk of a huge oak and find the woodbine there and brush it with brilliant red, and what I have left over I spread across the outer oak leaves. I fling a gauzy curtain of blue-gray over the hills and I paint the meadows gold and beige and trim them with shades of leftover green. I tell the dogwoods to turn their berries to a bright red and their leaves to all shades of pink and green. I curl the bark from the cottonwood or the sycamore and watch it drift down a slow moving creek. The Creator put me to work at the beginning of time and I have never given it up. Each season gives me reason to renew and to think how I can make things more beautiful. Yellow is my favorite color, but then so is red and green and blue and all the others that I have so lavishly supplied to me. Come walk with me and the deer and the wild turkeys and all my other friends, and let us share the faith of the Creator.*

We are two-legged as the birds are because the birds leave the world with their wings, and we one day leave it in the spirit.

—PLAINS INDIAN

The past is ripe with wisdom and knowledge— if we are willing to reflect on it. Reflection brings to the heart all the reasons for things we did not understand earlier. Search among your memories for the sharp places that hurt so much that you buried them, as though in a grave.

Long ago shame whispered to you to hide your painful memories; now wisdom invites you to use them for good. Once you thought it was important to keep these experiences hidden—but no longer. Free yourself by taking those old humiliations and use them like keys to open your treasure boxes for a more beautiful and healthy life. A poet once wrote that the past is nothing but a bucket of ashes. But remember, the phoenix—elegant, beautiful, and powerful—rises from the ashes of past into the fullness of the present. You, too, can rise from the past and live fully now.

No man should seek to destroy the special genius that race ancestry give him.

—QUANAH PARKER, COMANCHE

OCTOBER

HARVEST MONTH

DUNA NA DEE'

OCTOBER 1

A thing of beauty is a joy forever," Keats wrote. Grace is a thing of beauty; it is a gift. My mother had that gift. Her apron may have been faded, her hair twisted into a knot on the back of her head, but she had a gracious quality that everyone respected.

One of the basic principles of grace is gentle concern for others, a willingness to hold up the one that cannot stand alone. My mother's unerring grace was never to look down on someone or to look up to status or guile. She looked everyone in the eye without judging. That is a grace that we can all strive for.

The life of an Indian is like the wings of the air.

—BLACK ELK, OGLALA SIOUX

Y ou stirred up your own emotions when you did not want to. You kept the faith when it seemed not to matter. You got up when you wanted to lie down. You were weak but you claimed strength. You were resentful, but you reached outside that resentment and took hold of something that erased all resentment. You overcame the melancholy mood not because you thought you could, but because you alone could not. You refused to listen to the persistent voices of wrong and took a strong grip on that which lifts and secures. You made it when everything seemed to defy the possibility. Some part of every victory stays you at every point where you will never again sink below it. You hung on for dear life, and there is no turning back now. The Spirit has been with you and will continue to be with you. Remember and give thanks.

As I prayed, I was aware of something above me and there he was; Earthmaker....

—WINNEBAGO

OCTOBER 3

Give others the benefit of doubt. Never imagine that someone has wronged you because of the way things look. Appearances deceive even the smartest people. Check things out. What is the truth?

Sometimes people do things that we don't think they should do. We can't definitely know what motivated them to do what they did—just as they can't know what definitely motivated us to do a particular thing. So why question motives that we cannot possibly know? Save yourself the pain and frustration of imagining that others have wronged you. If you seek it, the truth will come because you cared enough to look for it.

Indians have principles of truth, honesty, generosity, equity, and brotherhood.

—CHIEF LUTHER STANDING BEAR, LAKOTA

OCTOBER 4

Paths are dappled with soft October sunlight, and the grass has caught all colors of leaves. Breezes blow warm and cool, and a downy woodpecker raps on a tree and squawks at a squirrel. It is autumn, and fawns with spots only partially gone stand and watch a passerby with little fear.

A certain quietness falls on the land as plants go dormant and trees shed their leaves. Stand under a tree, and it becomes a shower of color that is gradually letting in more and more sunlight. Walk every chance you have to absorb the serenity and peacefulness of this season. It moves so fast, and we suddenly find ourselves in another season before we have enjoyed this one. Let it pace your heart and lower your blood pressure. It will sweeten your thought and soften your voice as a gift from God.

O ye people be you healed.

GOOD EAGLE, SIOUX

OCTOBER 5

Nothing has been used and misused as often, and nothing can save the day, like a good word. A word is power-packed, whether we read it or speak it or hear it. We command and we are commanded by the use of that power.

How often children are robbed of self-confidence and good feelings about themselves because someone strikes out and destroys with unthinking words. Sick people are made sicker by negative talk around them, although it seems they sleep. Relationships have been shattered and prosperity dissolved because of the choice of words.

Because of their awesome power, listen carefully to your words—and watch carefully what words of others you listen to. Choosing words—and listening—wisely strengthen you and others as well.

We are as well-behaved as you and you would think so if you knew us better.

AHENAKEW, CREE

OCTOBER 6

A voice in our ear pleads for us to pay attention. Listen closely, see with the eyes of the mind. So much will pass us by if we are asleep! No need to go blank in your mind, no need to stay motionless. Go on with your work and keep your mind open to ideas and to the brightness of each new day. Many beautiful things wait to be discovered if only we could open to them. Instead we open to foolishness and to all the rumors and hearsay that are not ours to use. Let tension melt away when you turn from your worries and lay a gentle hand on someone to comfort them. Smile and laugh when you have the least reason. It is the grace that opens new doors—not outward, but inward where all the hurts once held sway but now are released.

All birds, even those of the same species, are not alike, the same with animals and human beings.

—SHOOTER, TETON SIOUX

OCTOBER 7

If you feel insecure, make yourself aware of what real security is. True security is more than a life-long work, more than having familiar surroundings and trustworthy people around you. True security comes in being one with the Spirit.

Greed and self-importance will threaten your spiritual security. How do you respond? Just open your spiritual eyes: see your protection and feel its warmth. Remember "underneath are the everlasting arms." Spiritual power exists, but you cannot claim it until you recognize the source from which it comes. Open yourself to the power of the Spirit. Only then will you feel truly secure.

You can count your money and burn it within the nod of a buffalo's head but only the Great Spirit can count the grains of sand.

—NORTHERN BLACKFEET

OCTOBER 8

On rare occasions you may have felt a word drop into your heart that you knew meant something because it never faded and always stood as a reminder that something profound happened. You may not have understood then, but your mind has gone back to it numerous times wondering what it meant.

Years can pass between an event and the understanding of it. It may be we have to grow up to it, or that our minds and spirits have to mature enough to see how it is to play out in our lives. It is little different from building a house—you can see the structure going up, but you know it can't be used until it is finished. Sometimes ideas and visions need time to firm up before we can use them.

The child was encouraged not to grow lazy and to grow straight like a sapling.

—MOURNING DOVE, SALISH

OCTOBER 9

What person does not hope for a spiritual experience that will connect him with the inevitable Source of all good? What person does not hope for a touch of the Divine to open his stony heart to understand his own potential?

But what happens to our deep spiritual longing in the face of catastrophic world events? Many people will claim that that's just the way the world is; there's nothing we can do about it. But that negativity propels those people—and the world—further toward destruction. What can we do? It is our very personal responsibility to counter that negativity. Our deep spiritual longing reveals that we have tasted the spirit in our lives and we hunger for more. The world also hungers for a taste of the Spirit—and it is that which will keep us all from destruction. Let us draw on Spirit to guide us in sustaining all of creation.

When the Earth is sick, the animals will begin to disappear. When that happens, the Warriors of the Rainbow will come to save them.

—CHIEF SEATTLE, SUQUAMISH

OCTOBER 10

Tiny moss pads decorate the path to the woods. Bright green and glistening like pins in a pincushion, they thrive where earlier there seemed to be no life at all. The same potential rests in us, if we could only believe.

Springtime feathers the wild plum in a profusion of fragrant blooms, but now it stands in dormant roughness until its season is due. Other trees are individually lighted with brilliant oranges and reds, and the sumac lies in groves of burgundy and crimson.

Each tree and each growing thing stands in its place and looks like everything else, until its season comes to stand in the light. The same privilege is ours if we stand faithfully and eagerly expect our season to come. Wait for it, and it will surely come.

To make medicine is to engage upon a period of fasting, thanksgiving, prayer, and thanksgiving.

—WOODEN LEG, CHEYENNE

OCTOBER 11

There should be a clearinghouse in our minds to tell us in no uncertain terms that we don't need to know everything there is to know. Too much of today's information is trash. We learn things that we only have to unlearn later when we discover they are either not true or do not apply to us.

We are willing listeners, convinced that if we experience something, we can grow by it. Experience may have taught us a few things, such as not to put our hands in the fire and not to stand in traffic. But gathering experience by taking in endless information may not be good for us. Exposing our minds and hearts to filth is not only a waste of time and effort, it is also a waste of spirit. So judge carefully when you take in information—let it go if it is not good or necessary. Keep your mind fresh for things of the Spirit.

When a child, my mother taught me the legends of the people, taught me of the sun and sky, the moon and stars, the clouds and storms.

—GERONIMO, APACHE

OCTOBER 12

Get up out of the ashes—this is no time to give up. If you think you are a lost cause and nothing can help you, fight those thoughts. You haven't even begun to see what changes can be made in your life.

What should you do? First of all, remove the "rock" from your head. The "rock" is any burden, imagined or real. If you need to be forgiven, ask for it. If you need to make amends with someone, make them—but never let that martyr complex take over. Push regret, sorrow, and guilt aside, because they can destroy you. Make a "safe house" within your soul. Do not strike out in a destructive passion. And last but not least, ask the Spirit for relief, because when you ask in faith, you will receive—and you will know that you are never a lost cause.

The purpose is to subdue the passions of the flesh and improve the spiritual self.

—WOODEN LEG, CHEYENNE

OCTOBER 13

Take an eraser to your mind the way you would to a blackboard. Remove all the ugly memories and all the shoulds and oughts that have ruled from many times past. Stand free of prejudices and allow yourself to care about gentleness and kindness and love. Stop stumbling over calories and fat and no money, no friends, and very little self-confidence. Destroy the mean streak and envy. Shake loose and get away from the stiffness, the plastered down, the weepy.

How would it feel to simply be free? How would it be to never have another ailment? Walk free and live free the way you were meant to be. Never, never think these things are impossible.

The Great Spirit is our Father, but the earth is our Mother.

—BEDAGI, WABANAKI

OCTOBER 14

L ife is like a fresh spring that flows strong and clear—and then puddles in those hard-to-cross places. The spring catches debris and sometimes it is easily riled—but it can clean itself and move on.

Sometimes we clog the spring of our lives with fear, weariness, and a faith that is so shaky it cannot sustain us when we need it most. Doubt clings like a cloud on an autumn day, and we question if we are supposed to do anything worthwhile. But remember the spring that cleans itself and moves on. We can do the same. How? Throw out worry and take up a new life, the same way you bite into a fresh fall apple. Taste the tangy sweetness and let the juices run where they will. Look at a single flower and revel in its perfection and fragrance. Give yourself the gift of freedom—for one hour, one day, one lifetime. It only takes a beginning. Why not begin now?

You will have to dig down through the soil to find nature's earth. The upper part is Crow.

—CURLEY, CROW

What makes us look with greedy eyes on something that won't mean a thing after a few hours? We strained toward it, we thought it would give us joy. But now we find it hard to live with—and we wonder how we ever could have wanted it so badly. Greed is a frightful enemy, an enchanting siren song that can lure us into dark ports. Watch and be wise.

The wisdom we need in order to face greed is not just human wisdom. We must have spirit wisdom, which reaches far beyond our illusions about what is real and what isn't, what we need and what we don't, what will satisfy us and what won't. Trust that spirit wisdom is available to you. Simply ask and it will be given.

Give me the strength to walk the soft earth…the eyes to see…and the strength to understand.

—BLACK ELK, OGLALA SIOUX

OCTOBER 16

Sweet is the peace and serenity of the early morning before anything makes a harsh sound or shakes the morning dew. Two deer feed along the woodland path, and a red leaf or two float down from the woodbine. Autumn begins to settle in and the cool quiet of morning mists soothe the spirit.

Human spirits need a lift now and then. But it is not the things outside a person that turn on the light or heal the soul. Only the heart can do that. The heart is the core, a place where words, beliefs, and images are stored. Life springs from this place and rejects the darkness, no matter how many times it presents itself.

Be like the flower that opens to the light and closes when touched by darkness. The choice is yours—the darkest night cannot touch the bloom that will not open to it.

All their wisdom and knowledge came to them in dreams.

—CHIPPEWA ELDER

OCTOBER 17

Last night the rain came. It wasn't as much as we needed, but it was much appreciated. The moonflower bloomed profusely—eight huge blossoms like spotlights glowed in the dark, showing its gratitude for the moisture. That was a gift. Another gift came when we watched a bundle of brown fur descend the long rock walk to the woods: a rock-chuck came up to investigate the change in temperature. We have seen rock-chucks sunning on the huge boulders at the foot of the cliff, but this is only the second time we have seen one near our house.

Sometimes when we don't get what we think we need (like our thinking we needed a lot of rain), we receive gifts we don't expect: the grace of a little rain, the beauty of a blooming moonflower, and the delight of a roving rock-chuck. Perhaps those were the gifts we *really* needed, and the Spirit, who is much wiser than we, generously gave them to us. May we have the wisdom to receive those unexpected gifts with thanks and deep appreciation.

With your power only can I face the winds.

—BLACK ELK, OGLALA SIOUX

OCTOBER 18

We prefer constant movement to waiting. But waiting gives us time to rest, to prepare, to build up the spirit, to make ourselves ready for what lies ahead. Waiting creates staying power so that there is no need to retreat—or, as the Cherokee put it, *a si ni*, "no need to go backward." We need to remember that waiting is only a prelude to action, even though as we wait, we may not know what kind of action it is that lies ahead of us.

Waiting is a power-gathering time, so when we finally see what it is that we must do or where it is that we must go, we will have the strength to face any challenge. Waiting allows the body, mind, and spirit to become balanced and ready to work together. And when mind, body, and spirit work as one, we can move mountains. So do not fear waiting—it can be a spirit gift.

The path to Glory is rough and many gloomy hours obscure it.

—BLACK HAWK, SAUK

OCTOBER 19

John Burroughs said that we can fail many times, but we don't really fail until we blame someone else for what we've done or haven't done. Once we fail we tend to think we can do nothing right. We condition ourselves to fail when we relive what happened in detail over and over again. The only real losers are the ones who call themselves losers and deny there is any help. We change by saying we are changed and then acting on what we've said. Speak the true word to yourself and stop looking for sympathy. Don't be buddies with those who believe nothing is good. Shake off excuses and go free. Being free is worth everything we put into it.

Good words do not last long unless they amount to something.

—CHIEF JOSEPH, NEZ PERCE

OCTOBER 20

The hills of autumn have a smoky look, a blue haze that hangs suspended along the horizon. On a sunny day, the sumac and woodbine vie for the brightest shades of burgundy and red. When the clouds move in the colors are muted and blended like an artist's oils, and no less beautiful. Sound, when there is any, vibrates on the ear like faraway music. The only continuous noises are the twigs and crisp leaves that crunch beneath the feet. And then comes the surprise of a wild gobbler calling the hen turkeys to follow. The sun is warm, the air cool, the fragrance of wood smoke wafts through the woods.

Nothing compares to autumn in the quiet woods. All other seasons have their pleasant qualities, but peace is a special quality of autumn. It is time for praise and thanksgiving—a time for saying blessings over this land and its rich harvest.

While we sat watching the herd, father said, "These horses are godlike, or mystery beings."

—WOLF CHIEF, HIDATSA

OCTOBER 21

Someone said that if our capacity to acquire has outstripped our capacity to enjoy, we are on our way to the scrap heap. If that it true, it seems that many of us are headed for the scrap heap. Why is it we collect so many things—clothes, TVs, cars, toys for the kids and grandkids, and on and on? Are we so empty inside that we have to keep trying to fill ourselves up—but nothing works?

So how do we get things into balance? First, simply stop—stop buying, gathering, amassing. Most of us have plenty of stuff. Second, reflect on what you want and what you truly need. Third, consider sharing what you have with others. Fourth, take some quiet time each day. Go for a walk. Look out the window at your garden. Hold a kitten. Do something you really enjoy doing—and let yourself enjoy it fully. Finally, ask the Spirit to help you to truly enjoy life each moment of the day. Ask and you will receive.

You might as well expect rivers to run backwards as any man born free be contented penned up.

—CHIEF JOSEPH, NEZ PERCE

OCTOBER 22

When planting herbs from the garden of a friend, Sir Francis Bacon said, "A perfect garden with herbs, when trod upon, gives the very air a delightful fragrance." Kneeling to plant herbs, digging in the soft warm earth with our hands, feeling the warm sun on our backs—what small things these are, and yet they are not small at all. Such small things, simple things are often very important to our physical, spiritual, and mental well-being. We have no idea how healing comes seeping in through those times, those moments when we let go of worry, focus on small tasks, and simply feel thankful.

The voice of the Great Spirit is heard in the twittering of the birds, the rippling of mighty waters, and the sweet breathing of the flowers.

—ZITKALA SA, YANKTON SIOUX

If you want to walk on water you're going to have to get out of the boat. The boat represents the place of security—so easy to cling to the idea of security even though the actual boat may be flimsy. What "boat" don't you want to get out of— a familiar but dead-end job, a bad but steady relationship, the belief that you can't do something?

We all have things (and sometimes people) that we cling to for security. Security in and of itself is not bad, but it can become destructive if it keeps us from becoming who we truly are, if it keeps us from listening to our spirits, if it keeps us in bad situations or relationships. Take a careful look at what gives you security—and then ask yourself, "Do I need to get out of this boat?" It takes some real faith to step out of the boat, but if you really need to do it, you can—with Spirit's help.

I knew every stream and every wood. I have lived like my fathers before me, and like them, I have lived happily.

—TEN BEARS, COMANCHE

OCTOBER 24

Let me be your friend. I must have your permission to be a true friend, just as you must have my permission. But what does that mean? It means that we respect each other's privacy and honor each other's trust. Being a friend does not necessarily give permission to ask any and all questions. Curb the desire to know until your friend gives you permission to ask those super-personal questions. Your friendship may need to grow closer and with a deeper sense of trust before your friend will open all aspects of his or her life to you.

What does it take to be a true friend? A true friend knows how to touch without violating, to love without smothering, to care without constant pursuit, to give freely without wanting an immediate return. A true friend also cares enough to defend a friend against unfair comments, to stand alongside a friend during a time of crisis. Friends are not jealous or envious, nor are they judgmental. For a friend, no thanks are needed—just love.

A child is the greatest gift from Wankan Tanka.

—HIGH EAGLE

OCTOBER 25

The winner carries with him the quiet knowledge that though he has heard every argument, faced every opponent, felt every criticism, there is no turning back and no accepting defeat. Telling a winner that something is impossible is like waving a red flag—*a ga da ti*. He insists on going ahead, learning all he can about the challenges he faces and then persisting until there is nothing left to do but win. Every winner knows in his heart that he is not alone. His spirit and his dream merge so that even a loss will only be a delay. What we put into an idea, what we dream it can be, what we believe in and work toward is likely to make it take shape.

The Indian lived, lived to his last breath.

—CHIEF LUTHER STANDING BEAR, LAKOTA

OCTOBER 26

After a long dry spell, what could be as satisfying as the rumble of thunder declaring the end of a drought? Rain, like a gauzy gray curtain, sweeps across the valley and raps on the roof, and the desire to stand at the window and watch is overpowering. The rain after a period of drought is a great blessing.

Blessings come in many ways and after many different kinds of "droughts." For the drought of loneliness, there is the blessing of the preacher who stays to talk; for the drought of sadness, there is the blessing of the friend who makes you laugh; for the drought caused by conflict, there is the blessing of peace that comes with the gentle-spirited; and for the drought of the blues, there is the blessing of those who cheer others. Who do you know who might be experiencing a drought of some kind? What kind of blessing, what kind of rain can you be?

The earth is under the protection of something which at times becomes visible to the eye.

—LONE MAN (ISNA-LA-WICA), TETON SIOUX

322

Be quiet and refuse to talk about your trouble. Stop and be grateful—just say how grateful you are and there will be more for which to be grateful.

We were given the ability to count our blessings or good fortunes, but instead we count all the wrong things. Sure, there are experiences in life that aren't the best, but we are not supposed to give them glory. Bad experiences, hurts, and all the feelings that go with them will diminish us if we let them. When we keep telling everyone about them, we leave no room for happiness or contentment. If all the space is taken up with what is wrong, how can we grow and become good? How can we see beauty? How can we see anything to love?

Stop thinking about trouble. Start giving thanks and rest easily knowing that any pain you have is being dissolved.

[The Spirit] sang its spiritual song for the child to memorize and use when calling upon the spirit guardian as an adult.

—MOURNING DOVE, SALISH

OCTOBER 28

We are human, and human beings tend to judge by how they feel. But our feelings are not reliable. Feelings ebb and flow—they are not steady. Observe your feelings for a while, and see how they move back and forth: they flow this way with good news, and that way with bad. We know how easily bad feelings can trap us in self-pity. Forlorn and wretched, we feel abandoned, blue. The blues come from mismanaged emotions—relying on everything negative rather than being of good courage. Manage your emotions by focusing on the positive—and your life will run much more smoothly.

Every spirit wants to look his very best when he goes to meet the Great Spirit.

—WOODEN LEG, CHEYENNE

OCTOBER 29

Time, time, time. Everyone worries about time: When is this due? How much time will it take? How long will we have to wait?

Ironically, despite all our rushing around, we seem to do a lot of waiting. It's the old hurry-up-and-wait syndrome. Waiting takes up so much of our time, and it seems like a terrible waste. But in reality, all those times of waiting are just as important as all our rushed attempts to be somewhere or do something on time. Times of waiting, of shifting into neutral, are times we can call our very own—time to think out a problem, time to watch events unfold, time to pray, even if we have not prayed before.

So the next time you have to wait, take a deep breath and thank Spirit for waiting. Open up to your waiting and see what gifts it gives you.

We believe that Wankan Tanka is everywhere.

—CHASED-BY-BEARS, SANTEE SIOUX

Harmony, think harmony, and never react to criticism. Most people believe they know what you are all about, but they do not. Disraeli told us it is much easier to be critical than it is to be correct. Remember that when you face the criticism of others—and when you are ready to criticize someone yourself. It is best never to criticize others. Give others the respect you expect for yourself.

With the help of the Spirit, we have reached a ripe old age.

—BLACK ELK, OGLALA SIOUX

Once we have been afraid of something, it is easy to feel that fear again. It hangs in the back of the mind like an insect caught in a swinging fragment of spider web. Although the same experience may not come again, even the possibility of it terrorizes us.

Fear is the magician's wand that stirs the brew of all our negative feelings. Because fear is so powerful, we learn early on to push it out of sight so we do not have to handle it. But pushing fear out of sight does not resolve it. Instead, we need to acknowledge our fear and then handle it with words of faith. Tell fear you won't tolerate its distorting your emotions. Telling fear that it is unacceptable can bring a quiet balance. Say it often enough, and you eliminate the very makings of fear.

When I am too old and feeble to follow my sheep or cultivate my corn I am going to sit in the house and carve cachena dolls.

—TALAYESVA, HOPI

NOVEMBER

BIG TRADING MONTH

NU DA NA 'EGWA

NOVEMBER 1

We learn the hard way that time for ourselves is all-important. Personal time is as necessary as eating right, resting well, and refusing to admit negative thoughts. Quality time is far more important than large quantities of time. How we use what we have makes all the difference.

Even a walk in the woods or in a park, or lunchtime spent near a flowing fountain can refresh; a weekend away may be a real treat. Quality time, for many people, also means quiet time—sitting, praying, or perhaps doing some kind of needlework or artwork that is calming and quieting.

Pay attention to what nourishes you in your personal time—then find ways of incorporating that into your schedule. When you take care of yourself, you will find not only that your life is more enjoyable but also that you make life more enjoyable for others as well.

The Great Spirit created this country for the use and benefit of his red children.

—BLACK HAWK, SAUK

NOVEMBER 2

Spirit, mind, and body—all need peace and quiet. We need a quiet place like a creek bank in summer when fishing is good and bait plentiful. The mind and spirit need to go fishing in the inner world of thought and ideas. When the body is quiet, the mind can pull in some big ones, but do be careful. Good fish and not-so-good fish can come out of the same pool. Rely on the spirit to guide you to the good—and to help you distinguish between the good and the bad. Throw the bad ones—bad ideas, bad words, bad beliefs—away. But the good ones are keepers. Savor them.

[We] must always follow the directions of the Great Spirit, and we must listen to him, as it was he that made us: determine to listen to nothing that is bad.

—TENKSWATAYA, SHAWNEE

NOVEMBER 3

Can I convince you of your great importance? You are the captain of your personal ship, the guide to your greatest dream. See yourself the way you want to be. See yourself as a giver and a receiver. Look for ways to be wiser and not sorry. Find the path to happiness that is your spirit. Too few have heard their own praises lauded. No one thinks to tell you how much you mean to them. Remember, you have to be kind to yourself so that you can be kind to others. If you have to go back to childhood to recall being loved, do so. Think how wonderful it was to share in something called love and kindness. If it was not there, then put it there in your heart. Never tell yourself you are not worthy, because you are more worthy than you will ever know. No one was put on this earth by accident, but for a purpose. Find that purpose and be who you want to be.

We looked up to the Great Spirit.

—BLACK HAWK, SAUK

NOVEMBER 4

Wait for wisdom, wait with patience. Never let a microwave mentality take over your life. Wait for the right time. Remember, the things you want will come to you if you wait.

John Burroughs once made an interesting comment about waiting. He said we should be patient but that we should also "hustle" while we wait. What does that mean? It means be prepared, have things in order, tie up loose ends, and get rid of negative thoughts. So waiting doesn't necessarily mean sitting around and doing nothing. It means preparing ourselves—in body, mind, and spirit—even if we don't know what we're preparing for.

If you are willing to wait for as long as it takes, then your wait will not be long.

The man who sat on the ground in his tipi meditating on life and its meaning, accepting the kinship of all creatures, and acknowledging unity with the universe of things was infusing into his being the true essence of civilization.

—CHIEF LUTHER STANDING BEAR, LAKOTA

NOVEMBER 5

When time is short and there's a lot to do, don't say you can't do something. Start out in faith, and when you get into the flow of what needs to be done, strength and wisdom come.

Starting out in faith is the most important step. If you wait until everything is right, you can forget 95 percent of what you were going to do. There's never a "perfect" time to do anything, and there's never a flag that tells you when to start running. So, just take a deep breath and start out in faith—and ignore all the signs that tell you you're never going to make it. You will make it. Those who start out in faith, end up with the prize.

Formerly, when we lived in ignorance, we were foolish; but now, since we listen to the voice of the Great Spirit, we are happy.

—TENKSWATAYA, SHAWNEE

NOVEMBER 6

We all handle hundreds of decisions every day—dress or pants, cereal or pancakes, coffee or tea, this project or that, shopping or banking, park here or there, and so on. If we really knew how many decisions and details we attend to each day, we'd be overwhelmed. Sometimes we're overwhelmed even without knowing the exact number! But few decisions are more important than this one: what words we use with those around us. Even on our busiest day, we can find time to say, "Great job!", "What a lovely dress!", "Thank you!", and most important of all, "I love you!" Remember to keep life and love at the top of the list of decisions you have to make each day. You'll be happier, and others will be too.

Is not kindness more powerful than arrogance; and truth more powerful than the sword?

—CHIEF LUTHER STANDING BEAR, LAKOTA

When we're under stress, we think we should know everything. We know that somewhere in the back of our minds we have all the answers to what confronts us, but no matter how hard we try, we can't find the answer we need. We won't be able to as long as we're under stress.

Ironically, the best thing we can do in situations like this is walk away! Many dilemmas are solved the minute we put them down and leave them. If we let the problem loose, we often find that the solution emerges effortlessly. So loosen up, let go, turn your attention to something totally different. Relax and the answers will come.

Any one could pray to the spirits, receiving answer usually in a dream.

—EDWARD GOODBIRD, HIDATSA

Have you ever had a good idea that just keeps coming back to you? Maybe you don't quite know what to do with it. When you try to push it away, the idea keeps coming back. When that happens, it's time to pay attention! There's a reason this idea keeps coming back to you—probably because Spirit keeps bringing it back to you.

Try talking with it. You may be amazed at what you'll learn. Take a notebook and simply ask the idea, "Why do you keep coming back to me?" and then wait for an answer. Write that answer down and ask another question. Before long, you have a regular conversation going with the idea. Some call this intuition, some simply an urge, and some believe the idea speaks from their own subconscious. Wherever it comes from, pay attention— because this idea may be leading you to new and better things.

Slowly I perceived that a voice was trying to tell me something. It was a bird cry, but I tell you, I began to understand some of it.

—JOHN (FIRE) LAME DEER, LAKOTA

on't study the problem, study the solution. Whatever the problem is, remember that spirit is part of the solution. Emerson said, "Great men are they who see that the spiritual is stronger than any material force." No matter how difficult or complex a problem is, Spirit knows and cares about the solution. As important as the intellect may be in finding a solution, remember that intellect will never overcome the spirit any more than pride can overcome humility. That does not mean you shouldn't use your intellect, but it does mean you shouldn't try to solve a problem by intellect alone. Open yourself to Spirit, and Spirit will lead you to the solution.

The monitor within my breast has taught me the will of the Great Spirit.

—SENACHWINE, POTAWATOMI

If you are at a point where nothing comforts you, take heart—there are answers. But those answers are not in a pill or in what others say and do. The answer lies within you—or more precisely, in what you say and do. Begin now by removing everything negative from what you say and do—no matter how much you want to say or do it. Quiet yourself and avoid talking. Avoid telling others what you are doing, because many will not want you to be freed from your misery—they want you to be miserable just as they are.

As you remove the negative from your life and as you quiet yourself, you will create a place within you where peace can dwell. Peace must have an invitation to enter your heart, otherwise it cannot come in. Your efforts to move toward quietness and away from negative are that invitation. Trust that now you will receive the peace you long for.

I do not want war at all, but want to make friends, and am doing the best I can for that purpose.

—SATANTA, KIOWA

NOVEMBER 11

We can go inside our minds and close the door so tightly that we can't get out and nothing good can get in. It is not a good life when thought and attention are so riveted on what is wrong that nothing good can be seen.

Do you want a full life? Then let go of negativity and claim the Living Words of life. Do you want a full life? Then let go of ingratitude and give thanks. Do you want a full and victorious life? Then close the door on trouble and say, "I will reach for the all that promises fullness of life."

Now that I am to speak, the sun, the moon, the earth, the air, the waters, the birds and beasts, even children unborn shall rejoice at my words.
—CHIEF COCHISE, CHIRICAHUA APACHE

NOVEMBER 12

The reason we are so afraid of not having government funding is because we have no confidence in being able to take care of ourselves. When the first help came, it was met with gratitude. When the second help arrived, it changed something inside us. We began to say, "If we can get someone else to do it, why should we?"

All our lives we have looked for someone to take care of us, someone to lean on, to use as a packhorse, a caretaker, an unpaid servant. The thought of being responsible scares the daylights out of us. But once we commit ourselves to being responsible, what an amazing change it makes in our spirits. Strength comes along with independence and happiness. We are worthy.

We never did the white man harm, we don't intend to.

—TALL BULL, CHEYENNE

Nothing is set forever in one direction. Change is part of life, but once we have found the right course in life, we must stay on it. To do that, we must desire to stay on the right course and be constantly attentive to that course.

But staying on the course won't necessarily be easy. All along the way we will face potholes and pitfalls, and we must pay attention so we don't fall into them. When we stay focused on our direction, every step we take, everything we do keeps us on course. But if we lose our focus, if we listen to voices from the past whispering that we've made a lot of mistakes and will never find the right way, we may in fact lose our way. But we can whisper back and tell all those negative voices to get lost. Then, as we continue on, we express our gratitude every day that we are on the right course.

From all quarters we receive speeches from the Americans, and not one is alike. We suppose they intend to deceive us.

—BLUE JACKET, SHAWNEE

NOVEMBER 14

When a name or a word we want to recall does not come, it is so easy to throw up our hands and say we can't remember anything. Saying those words will help us forget because we keep reminding ourselves all the time. The traditional Cherokees had no problem with memory. It was their duty to remember what had happened so they could carry it on down the line to those who did not know. Sometimes these persons were called the storytellers, because they kept records in their brains that were no longer written anywhere else.

Though today there may be electronic equipment to record all these facts, what if we are required to relate what we have collected but we have no electricity? Send for the one who has practiced remembering. This person may color the picture with certain tints and shades, but the facts are there. Time was given to seeing, sensing, tasting, and hearing. A wealth of wisdom can be tapped if we know where to look—and how to hear.

Take only memories, leave nothing but footprints.

—CHIEF SEATTLE, SUQUAMISH

S it quietly. Close your mouth and open your eyes. Be aware of everything going on around you. Hear the sounds, what are the colors? After a few seconds, everything becomes clearer. You are paying attention, which is important. It keeps a person out of the rumble of things, and the danger of saying the wrong things or talking too much is jerked out of the way like a wrinkled towel that snaps when you shake it so that it folds smoothly.

We must pay attention. If our mental and physical posture is in a slump, so are we. The Spirit cannot talk to us if we are not aware. But if we pay attention, if we really hear, some of the loveliest words, some of the most beautiful music seems to come out of nowhere to set us on a new path.

We thank the Great Spirit that all these wrongs now cease.

—SATANK, KIOWA

When things are bad, we're sure that what we are going through is the worst that anyone has ever experienced. Know that others have stood in this place, others have gone through what we're going through, and they made it free and clear.

The day will come when we can look back and ask ourselves, "What did this bramble bush of difficulty teach us?" The first thing is not to wait so long to take care of a problem, but the best thing is to be grateful and to say we are healed—even before we see proof that a healing has taken place and a stone has been lifted from our shoulders. Hope and faith can change difficulty in a way we can hardly believe. But as we look back on what happened in our lives, we see proof of this—and there are not enough words to say how wonderful it is.

The old Indian teaching was that it is wrong to tear loose from its place on the earth anything that may be growing there. It may be cut off, but it should not be uprooted. Trees and the grass have spirits.

—WOODEN LEG, CHEYENNE

Somewhere deep within us is a likeness to others that defies the most drastic difference we believe exists. If it were not so, we would know no compassion, feel no love, and have no understanding. It is true that we are very different. Perhaps you can't stand what and who I am, but on the other hand, I might not like you very much either. But that would be totally different if we were ever to get to know each other. Sometimes people aren't what we think they are—and we aren't what they think we are—because time has taught us to protect our vulnerability. But there is a spark of spirit that penetrates that protection, and it helps us say to the most unlikely person, "You poor unholy thing. I like you anyway." When we do, do we know that we are talking to ourselves?

We at once gave you our hearts. You now have them.

—SATANK, KIOWA

NOVEMBER 18

Elise, Cherokee grandmother, said, "Always look behind the stick that stirs." It will tell you if there is any truth in what is being touted. Ask yourself: What are people's motives? Who supports a certain idea or plan? Does something prosper or not?

Do not be fooled by what you see. Filter what you hear for worthless impurities, and go beyond your natural senses for deeper meanings and purposes. Keep your understanding free and observant, for there is much that will obscure it. Nothing is so exclusive that you cannot have access to the truth. And remember always to look behind the stick that stirs.

I say by the sun and the earth I live on, I want to talk straight and tell the truth.

—SATANTA, KIOWA

NOVEMBER 19

Anyone who has ever woven a basket, pieced a quilt, or painted a picture knows how satisfying it is to mix the colors and fibers and textures. One or two shapes or colors may not make a picture, but as more are added each day, more of the design is revealed.

Events are woven into life the same way. Some of the strands may be weak and some of the fibers seem colorless. There may be no real design, and we may find ourselves working with drab and unattractive pieces. Limited vision discourages us and makes us think we have not done one exciting thing.

Given time, we find the quiet tones of life, the times that seemed colorless are suddenly important and worth recalling. Excitement is a minor feature on the face of existence and is not the most important part of real living. But if we gather all that we have experienced in life, we will make a serviceable quilt and paint a picture of contentment. In short, we will make a good life.

I am the man that makes it rain.

—LONE WOLF, KIOWA

Curious, I watched a bird perched in the top of an oak tree that has only a smattering of leaves remaining. The bird sat very still. It seemed to turn its head so that its beak showed plainly. It should have moved more than it did because only an owl would sit that still, and it was too small to be an owl. I watched at intervals but nothing changed. A large number of blackbirds flew over and some of them landed in the tree. Was it a blue jay? Any other bird would have flown, but it did not. After awhile, I realized it was not a bird at all, no matter how much it had looked to be.

How many times have we judged something to be a certain way? Very often, things are not as they appear. We can be so sure and insist on what we think is real, and it isn't real at all. Our sight and our insight are tangled and we make a judgment that has no substance. How can any of us have accurate vision without the Spirit to guide us?

When I make peace, it is a long and lasting one— there is no end to it.

—SATANTA, KIOWA

NOVEMBER 21

Have you ever said you felt "foggy-headed"? Just like the morning fog that blurs the edges of the barn, the woods, the animals as we look out our window, mental fog hides the fine edges and full color of our lives. But just as the sunlight and warmth remove the haze that clouds the morning, it is the light and warmth of the Spirit that breaks through our fog and reveals the splendor of all. Then we hear the joyous music of life and it lifts us out of our lethargy.

The riches we have we cannot take with us.

—RED CLOUD, SIOUX

Ten Bears was an influential Comanche chieftain right after the Civil War. He was intelligent about a great many things and spoke fully about his people and their background. He said, "You…want to put us on a reservation and to build houses and Medicine lodges. I don't want them." He was born where there were no enclosures and everything drew a free breath. He wanted to die there, and not within walls.

What makes other people think they know what is best for us? The desire to live simply and happily is in most of our hearts. Human beings are not so complicated as today's conditions make them seem. If we crave things so much, why do we so easily discard them? Indians never had garage sales and they had no junk shops to sell their castoffs. They lived simple and uncluttered lives where they had time to think and ponder life.

We did not think of the great open plains, the beautiful rolling hills, the winding streams with tangled growth, as "wild."

—CHIEF LUTHER STANDING BEAR, LAKOTA

Start out in faith, but know the very act of faith brings challenges. No one cares when we sit in silence and do nothing. When actually doing something, taking a step forward, stirs the heart of envy.

Opposition is the first sign that we are doing something that should be done. No one else has had the courage to do it, but criticism doesn't take courage. Action takes courage.

If you want to move mountains, go move them. Don't let anything stop your good thoughts and constructive words. Even if you have to speak them to yourself quietly, do it. Not once, not twice—speak them over and over, and watch the thing happen. Listen intently and learn to discern what is there to help you—and what is meant to destroy.

I am glad that I have come here, and that we understand one another.

—RED CLOUD, SIOUX

NOVEMBER 24

When life becomes skewed and everything points to failure, stop right there and refuse to take in what is seen and sensed. Refuse to listen to talk that is down and out. Refuse to be one of the herd that panics every time the stock market dives. Turn to your own set of values and what you know to be true. Never trust anyone else's verdict, unless you are not on the right track. Never be a hot dog about anything you have not worked out for yourself. Watch your tongue and what you have been saying. Talking matters. What are you relying on? If it is appearance, you are riding for a fall. Do you know who you really are? Get to know, because it will count when you have a chance to perform and you can—or cannot. Know well what you have to work with and perfect it at every chance. Then you will be able to deal with whatever life brings.

You call the Great Spirit Jesus in your language; we call Him in the Crow language, E-so-swe-wat-se. I am going to light the pipe and talk to the Great Spirit.

—CHIEF BLACKFOOT, CROW

NOVEMBER 25

During the late evening hours in the country, a song of nature frequently rises in the woods and again from the prairie to the north. A chorus of coyotes, probably only three or four but sounding like dozens, yip and howl enough to stir up all the neighborhood dogs. But the woods are also full of silent walkers, and most of them are bigger than a coyote. It is simply not their nature to make a fuss, but they are just as important as the coyote. So it is with human beings. Some howl to demand attention. But the quiet ones walk on in their serene ways and live to be victors. They know it is not the noise but the action that gets them where they want and need to be.

We do not inherit the land, we borrow it from our children.

—NATIVE AMERICAN PROVERB

If you want to know the meaning of peace, go down to a little stream and sit quietly. Sense the timelessness. Watch the water as it ripples past roots and over stones, and know it is washing away stress and worry and unhappiness. Close your eyes and listen to the wind rustling the leaves, and hear a bird chirp or a squirrel bark. Be so quiet you can hear the deer's hooves dragging through a carpet of autumn leaves and the hoot of an owl in the dark part of the woods.

Be still and silence the fears that try to invade this time. Touch the earth and feel its rhythm and its vibrations. See how it restores itself after being turned upside-down. God made it for us, so receive it as a gift.

The Great Spirit made these mountains and great rivers for us, and all this Land.

—CHIEF BLACKFOOT, CROW

NOVEMBER 27

L ong ago I had a teacher who was nicknamed "Buffalo," partly because of her great shoulders clad in black crepe, but mostly because she threatened to whip shy students for going blank at the blackboard.

Years later she attended a school reunion. We assumed that the nickname would no longer fit, and that something soft and gentle would have taken the place of the harshness we'd known. We were wrong. She came with the same attitude, the same overbearing manner, and informed most of her former students that she did not remember them at all.

Whole lifetimes can be lived without learning the importance of kindness. We had the privilege of knowing we were right in our judgment, but the greater lesson was that we had learned gentleness and that a real buffalo—unlike this human one— was quite amiable.

Perhaps the hardest duty in the performance of parenthood was not so much to watch the conduct of their children as to be ever watchful of their own.

—CHIEF LUTHER STANDING BEAR, LAKOTA

NOVEMBER 28

A Cherokee elder once said, "Indian forgive, but Indian not forget." It was obvious by his tone that he was not carrying a grudge—but that only one broken trust is sufficient. Trust is fragile, and truth is necessary for building trust. Most people play fast and loose with the truth, believing that others are not intelligent enough to remember what really happened. Often people couldn't care less about the truth. They say, "It happened. OK, let's all forget it." But forgetting about the truth isn't the way—at least it's not the right way. We must be trustworthy, we must care. Truth and trust are beautiful gems. We must treasure them. When we do, the world will become a better place.

Agreements the Indian makes with the government are like the agreements between the hunter and the buffalo after it has been pierced with many arrows. All it can do is lie down and give in.

—CHIEF OURAY, UTE

One-track thinking absorbs energy and hides good ideas like thick fog. People want to think for themselves, and they should. A good thinker seeks input from sources that benefit what he is trying to accomplish. His ear is turned to the sound of something that will help. But be aware that not everyone is open in this way. Some people throw up guards against the truth if it goes against what they want to believe. They hotly protest that they know as much as anyone else, which may be true—but on different subjects.

Remember that if what you offer rings of or looks like truth, know that it may not be well received. The market is not flooded with takers for truth. But be diligent: some will be open to your help even though they may not be beating down your door.

Everyone is ignorant—but on different subjects.

—WILL ROGERS, CHEROKEE

NOVEMBER 30

Think long and hard before you give control of your life to something or someone. Never having to think for yourself and take care of yourself does not mean you are free from responsibility. The only thing it does mean is that you have fewer choices over which you have control.

Now is the time to think about controlling the choices in your life. It's very easy to give up control over many parts of our lives if we don't take care and pay attention to what is happening. There are enough things in our lives that dominate us without giving society and government control over life itself.

Consider the mess that things are in and stop looking for ease and freedom from responsibility. Rev up your thinking, doing, and voting. Let the world know you have a right to have control over your own life, to make choices about your own life. When you do this, your self-respect will become stronger. Never violate the sacredness of respect.

When we are poor we will tell you of it.

—CHIEF BLACKFOOT, CROW

DECEMBER

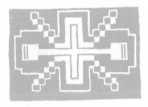

SNOW MONTH

U SKI'YA

DECEMBER 1

What we experienced yesterday does not form or shape our attitudes so much as what happened in childhood. Our beliefs, thoughts, and behavior patterns were formed in childhood and still hold the key to who we are today. Children are natural recorders, taking in minute detail and processing it for future use. If children regularly experience abuse and verbal cruelty, you can bet that they will, in turn, abuse and berate others.

But do our childhood experiences control what we do all of our lives, or can we change? We can definitely change if we really want to. We don't have to drag imperfections from the past into tomorrow. So it was there. It is not holy, and it has no blessing in it. Some ancestor may be cherished, but to preserve his imperfections as our own is wrong. Claim your own life and fill it with light and love worth recording in years to come.

I have worked with one heart and one object. I have looked ahead into the future and have worked for the children of my people.

—KICKING BIRD, KIOWA

DECEMBER 2

Walk in poison ivy and a rash will appear. Walk where all of life's laws are broken and trouble is assured. Laws are pure and simple. Break them and pay. Only the witless believe themselves above the law or too smart to get caught.

Laws, written and unwritten, are supposed to be for our good. If they are not, they are eventually repealed. But God's laws are set forever, and they serve as the foundation for every good act, every good outcome. Give people the opportunity to correct themselves, and if they don't, life itself will do the correcting. Things will be balanced, changes will be made, but it is the law of life that will win.

Among the Indians there have been no written laws. Customs handed down from generation to generation have been the only laws to guide them.

—CHIEF KAH-GE-GA-GAH-BOWH, OJIBWAY

DECEMBER 3

The Indian way to handle tension and worry is to spend time alone in meditation. Touch the earth and see the sky, look at the stars that you never in the world could count. Listen to the night bird sing and hear the tree toad's croaking song. Hear the hounds in the woods baying and the squalling of owls. These are basic things, common things, gentle things. Meditate on these. Close out the negative things of the world—the sensational and the shallow, the thoughtless words, offended airs, lofty attitudes. Let them pass as nothing, which they are. Close the door of your heart to all that is negative, and open it to the peace that passes all understanding. Let that peace rest your body, mind, and spirit.

Let everything be washed out, wiped out, and let there be no more blood.

—CAPTAIN JACK, MODOC

DECEMBER 4

Smoke rises from the river bottom where pecan groves have been cleared to make ready for the harvest. Fragrant air moves up gently and hangs like a blue curtain among the tallest trees.

Huge bales of gold-colored hay dot the meadows and suggest that one or two hard workers have a harvest. But the harvest is for everyone, according to what has been planted.

Seedtime and harvest also extend to what we have planted in thought, word, and action. The sower plants a word and it comes up in many different forms: hate, love, peace, patience. So be careful what you sow, because that is what you will reap.

The mocking bird said that it would take overnight to give them different languages. The mocking bird asked the chief if he would like to speak some other different language, but the chief said he would rather keep his own language.

—EDMUND NEQUATEWA, HOPI

Even with free choice, each of us has a tomorrow for which we are responsible. Never believe for a moment that you are free to meander across the world at random without influencing anything and anyone. No matter how misguided you may have been in the past, you have sensed there is something greater that loves and tries to help. Do not cut yourself off from Spirit help.

Emerson said there is no knowledge that is not power. Know that you have power, not over others but over yourself. If you believe you can overcome anything, you can overcome anything. Trust yourself and trust the Spirit to help you do what you were meant to do.

No longer should the Indian be dehumanized.

—CHIEF LUTHER STANDING BEAR, LAKOTA

DECEMBER 6

A terrified father found his small son wandering among strangers and scolded him, "I thought I told you to stay in the booth while I paid the check!" His teary reply was, "Daddy, I was trying to, but I don't know where it is."

Never assume anything. Don't assume that someone else understands what you mean or what you have pictured in your mind. Every person perceives differently. What seems to be absolutely clear in my mind may be absolutely clear in your mind, but it is not the same picture. We are unique individuals with sending and receiving ability in our heads. If we seem to communicate on most things, it is a miracle. Simple things that most of us take for granted can be staggering to others. We assume too much, ask too much, and don't take into account that everyone is not on the same wavelength. We need to remember this when we expect perfect performance.

It has been our wish to live here peaceably.

—SPOTTED TAIL, SIOUX

DECEMBER 7

New trends and new ideas interest all of us, but how we do love the familiar. We like to keep the things dear to us, the old songs, the familiar places, the good faces. Yet most of us have no desire to go back and recapture the old times—we have invested too much in what counts for us now.

At times, however, we get tired of bending toward the future. When something familiar comes to our ears or a certain fragrance touches our memory, then we recall a part of us that remains in the past. It's important to savor the familiar in the past, because sometimes that helps us to appreciate what we have today.

For it must be known that each man has his own peculiar song, and that he cannot sing that belonging to his comrade without this offering him an insult.

—NICOLAS PERROT, 1718

When we are really secure, we can let someone else have the credit for a success and not complain. Sooner or later the truth will surface, and when the truth is known, life balances the accounts. Sometimes it appears that someone is getting something for nothing, but Emerson said there is always compensation for good or for bad. We never do anything in secret for which we are not rewarded, nor do we escape the effect in our own lives. It is the reciprocal law of life that we get back what we send out to others. This requires us to do the best we can and leave the judgments and the balancing to that which works out all things to perfection.

Do you know who I am that you speak of me so?

—SITTING BULL, SIOUX

DECEMBER 9

Winter doesn't always come gradually. Sometimes it jumps on us with both feet, armed with ice and frigid winds that make the livestock hunt for cover and people shiver by the fire. We think how long and cold and mean and dangerous it is, and feel that winter will last forever. But it doesn't.

A time of adjustment comes with any change—whether that is a change of season or a change of life. Our grandmother used to say that our blood was too thin when winter began, but it would adjust and then it would warm us. We never knew if that was true, but we certainly hoped it was! Whatever comes, we adjust and go on. And one day, before long, the weather will change and we will be more comfortable. It's good to remember that at the beginning of winter and at other times of change.

All the savages who are not converted believe that the soul is immortal; but they maintain that when it is separated from the body it goes to a beautiful and fertile land, where the climate is neither cold nor hot, but agreeably temperate.

—NICOLAS PERROT, 1718

DECEMBER 10

We are creatures with needs that go deeper than what we work for daily. Especially at this busy time of year, we need to find some quiet time to be alone with ourselves. We need to be able to let down our guard and enjoy a moment when there is no pressure. As we let go of tensions and "to-do" lists, we begin to rest in body, mind, and spirit. Often quiet times like these refresh us more in a few short minutes than hours of sleep do. That's because here we let go to a far deeper rest—a spirit rest.

White people need a church house, a preacher, and a pipe organ to get into a praying mood. There are so many things to distract you....We think you can't have a vision that way.

JOHN (FIRE) LAME DEER, LAKOTA

DECEMBER 11

Slowly but surely things take shape and the long-awaited holidays are upon us. It always seems to take longer to prepare for the holidays than we think it should. And, of course, we want everything to be perfect—and it seldom is.

But if there is a perfect moment, a time when the meaning of this time truly comes home to us, all the work is worth it. Then we do not see the extra effort as a trial or burden. How could it be when our goal is to make someone happy, to show someone how much they are loved?

The reason for the survival of the Hopis has been our dedication to and faithfulness to our one God of the universe, and our adherence to our tradition and learnings.

—DAISY ALBERT, HOPI

DECEMBER 12

When something has been trying our souls, it is hard to come up and breathe fresh air. Something hangs a rock around our necks and we sag, droop, moan, and argue with frustration. How nice it would be to go to the garden, a plot of ground yielding fresh vegetables or an arbor covered with roses. But winter doesn't afford us such pleasures—unless we have captured the essence of these things in our minds to relive when we need them.

The need for a good memory is not just to recall a name or a face, but to bring what we need into vision. It is the Native American's way to go into a field of no particular beauty simply to pay attention. We mentally record the colors, the shapes, the birds and their songs, and then when we return to our homes, we recite to ourselves or others what we have seen. This sharpens memory and saves an experience that will come again when needed.

When the doctor does not know what medicine to use for a sick man the spirit of the plant tells him.

—CHEROKEE

Nutrition, or the lack of it, plays a large part in our ups and downs. What we feed our bodies goes hand in hand with what we take into our minds. Since mind, body, and spirit work together as a whole, we cannot ignore any part of ourselves and expect to get a good performance. We must be balanced in what we eat, in what we think, and in what we believe. And there's nothing wrong in asking for help in any of these areas—it's a sign of wisdom to do so. The rewards of asking are well worth the effort.

I want to tell you that our rations have been reduced to almost nothing. Many of our people have starved to death.

—SITTING BULL, SIOUX

DECEMBER 14

We all experience difficult moments in life when anything worthwhile seems far away. At those hard times, it pays to remember similar moments when we have doubted our ability to cope. As we look back, we realize that we did cope then, and life went on—many times in ways that we never expected. Difficult times, as hard as they may be to walk through, are not permanent. They cannot take away the best part of what we know and feel. The fact that we have known peace makes us know we will have it again—in greater portions, in sweeter times, in more lasting ways, because we are children of Spirit. We bloom like the flowers.

Time was divided into years and seasons; twelve moons for a year, a number of years by so many winters.

—JOHN QUINNEY, MAHICAN

DECEMBER 15

Sometimes we are nagged by the feeling that we are not getting. That feeling should remind us to remain steadfast and stay focused on our goal. A goal is achieved by the blending of time, effort, and, most of all, the belief in what we are working toward. When we have a worthwhile goal, we keep plugging along. Though every step may seem very small, when we look back we suddenly find we have covered a great distance. It is those little steps that get us where we are going. One by one they make progress, like drops of water eroding stone. Great strides impress us, but we seldom make them.

Remember the fable of the race between the hare and the tortoise: it was the one who was faithful and steadfast, the one who made small, steady steps, who reached his goal. You can do the same.

I was living peaceably and satisfied until people began to speak bad of me.

—GERONIMO, APACHE

DECEMBER 16

The old year is nearly gone, and if there could be one word that described it in general, it would be "complaining." People are so unhappy about so much, and they make it known through any avenue available to them.

There's nothing wrong with letting others know what isn't acceptable. But much complaining is simply that, and goes nowhere and accomplishes nothing. It gets to be just grousing and it only furrows the brow.

We were given freedom to speak our minds, but the freedom to do something doesn't mean it serves a good purpose. We could be using our voices, our words, to build and make amends, to encourage and enlighten. When we only complain, we waste a precious privilege and simply add to the turmoil.

We are all children of the one God. God is listening to me. The sun, the darkness, the winds, are all listening to what we now say.

—GERONIMO, APACHE

DECEMBER 17

What makes us believe everything we hear? So much is said to titillate, and so little of it means anything. This is the "he said–she said" syndrome, and truth to tell, none of it has any validity. Don't pass on gossip, because it will come back to haunt you, and you will know how silly you were.

While we're talking about talking, don't lie to save face, and don't hint at excitement that was never there. Avoid such foolishness. People who are wise never waste their time filling in blanks that were meant to be open and free. As the saying goes, "If you can't say something good, don't say anything at all." Just hunker down and wait. Your time will come, and when it comes (and it surely will) what you say will do good.

My brothers, the tongue of Kicking Bird is straight, and I cannot tell of all I saw.

—KICKING BIRD, KIOWA

DECEMBER 18

Writing about Christmas, E. B. White said, "To perceive Christmas through its wrapping becomes more difficult every year." Some people have no idea what Christmas really is, though the hunt for it has been incessant. For many, Christmas means spending more money than they can afford. Others feel that people expect too much—and they aren't going to give them anything. Still others have decided that Christmas means religion, and they refuse to be caught up in the materialism of the holiday season. All these things are the wrappings that E. B. White wrote about.

But there is a real Christmas. Christmas is supernatural power known as love. Call it whatever we will, it is and has always been supernatural, milk that turns into the richest cream. Look at it through the eyes of any denomination, it is still love. A life given for our redemption––so that we do not have to bear the results of all the things we've done—is a tremendous gift. It is the best gift we could ever receive.

The love of possession is a disease with them.

—SITTING BULL, SIOUX

DECEMBER 19

Laws govern everything. Written or unwritten, we have certain rules to keep if we are to do well and be happy. The law of music requires hitting the right notes if we are to hear a melody. Mathematics shows us the need for accuracy to solve problems. Faith is a law. We use faith even when we are not aware of it, or we disregard it and allow everything to turn out negative. A law is a law and serves us well when we avoid the sour notes and let the harmony come through. If we do not make music, it is our own fault, not the fault of the law. No one can take away our faith. If we lose it, it is because we let it go. Faith was born to open doors, to see beyond appearances, to forgive, to move us into new views that are immeasurable and unlimited. He said, "I did not come to destroy the law but to fulfill it." And so we do in myriad ways.

If there is but one religion, why do you white people differ so much about it?

—CHIEF RED JACKET, SENECA

DECEMBER 20

When we leave the old and familiar, something in us rebels. Even if it was not good, we recall bits and pieces that meant something to us. In leaving them behind, we leave a little of ourselves behind as well.

This seems to be a particular challenge around holidays. Our expectations of what a holiday should be like—even if we've never had one like that—are high. It takes courage and common sense not only to face our unrealistic expectations but also to shape new, more realistic ones. But it can be done—and you can do it. The Spirit will guide and strengthen you. Always trust the Spirit.

I will not be the first one to break this treaty.

—LITTLE RAVEN, ARAPAHO

DECEMBER 21

This is the time when we start to weigh and balance the year coming to an end. We reflect on what we did and didn't do, what things went well and what did not. We can learn both from what went well and what did not. Our challenge is not to let the things that didn't go well overpower us with guilt and grief. Yes, we need to acknowledge our mistakes and try to make amends where we can. But we also need to let the past be the past, and step on into the future. Leave behind the feelings that simply drag you down, then take the lessons you've learned this year into the future. They will serve you well.

The sky was the home of the god who held a watchful care over every star. They heard him whisper in the gentle breeze, or howl in the tempest.

—CHIEF KAH-GE-GA-GAH-BOWH, OJIBWAY

DECEMBER 22

When we were children, everything seemed magical. Now we are grown, and the light that revealed so much to us at that early age seems to be dimmer. And we look for it less. It is true that much has happened since we were children. We see more evil around us, and we are aware of what is going on in all parts of the world. Perhaps we feel more fear now that we are adults.

But during the time when people were fighting Indians, the Indians' fears were as great as ours are today. And here I am, an Indian, asking you not to be afraid. Trust that the events and situations of the world today will be tamed as other situations and events have been tamed in the past. Though we may not be able to see how, they will become part of life in the most ordinary ways and in the best ways. This is true because today, as it always has been, the One Spirit still reigns and in the Spirit lies our security.

We were seated on rich skins, of animals unknown to me, before the door of the Great Spirit.

—KICKING BIRD, KIOWA

DECEMBER 23

Our Creator blessed us with free will, and yet we cannot always see that we have options. When confronted with an obstacle, we can choose whether we explode in anger or take things in our stride. When the sun isn't shining, we can choose to love the rain.

We tend to look outside ourselves for help, but outside help isn't of much value if the Spirit is not within us. If we do not have the Spirit, we have a void within us that is greater than we can imagine. We need to invite the Spirit within, to honor it, and to listen carefully to it. When we begin to listen, we forget there is no sun.

The Great Spirit has given the white man great foresightedness; he sees everything at a distance, and his mind invents and makes the most extraordinary things.

—CROW BELLY, GROS VENTRE

DECEMBER 24

To accomplish anything, we have to have clearly defined goals and know how to break them down into easily handled segments. But first, goals have to be realistic. We are not going to lose twenty pounds in one day. We can't plant a garden and get it to bloom in one week. Second, goals are accomplished step by step, little by little. Even though most of us have much to do and too little time in which to do it, even five minutes a day can help us move toward accomplishing our goal. Too often we think we must have big blocks of time to accomplish anything, and as a result we don't do anything. So take five minutes today and see what you can do. And finally, the steps we take toward a goal come in an orderly sequence. One thing comes after another—and before you know it, you will have accomplished your goal!

When I was a child of five winters...I prayed to the spirits of animals, to the stars, the sun and the moon. My words were not many, but I prayed.

—POOR WOLF, GROS VENTRE

DECEMBER 25

My memories are filled with special people and the things they said, beautiful Christmas trees, and the smells of delicious food: homemade sausage sizzling in the skillet and the rich fragrance of coffee boiling on the wood range. My grandmother told me that drinking coffee would turn my knees black. I didn't worry about that because I suspected that by the time I climbed all the trees I wanted to my knees would be almost black anyway. I love the memory of Grandfather taking a bite of carrots, then widening his eyes and saying, "Now I can see so much better!" I knew he was pretending and the carrots still didn't taste any better to me, but I loved the charade and the laughter it caused. I loved Grandmother's hot biscuits and the love she baked in each one. But perhaps what I loved best was that Christmas was about the birth of a child—and I loved being a part of that child every day of my life.

He promised us he would return to the sky no more, that he would remain at the end of the earth and guide us to the ghosts of our fathers.

—KICKING BIRD, KIOWA

DECEMBER 26

We cannot lose what is truly ours and we cannot lose that which did not belong to us in the first place.

We must know that everything is balanced out with something, though just what may be difficult to detect at times. We have to believe that when one door closes, another one opens. As Emerson put it, "We cannot part with our friends. We cannot let our angels go. We do not see that they only go out that archangels may come in." So as hard as it may be, we need to let our "angels" go so that something greater can come to us. With time and faith, we may grow enough to accept something even greater. .

When they [the Sauk] imagine they have seen a ghost, the friends of the deceased immediately give a feast and hang up some clothing as an offering to pacify the troubled spirit of the deceased: they pray by singing over certain words before they lay down at night, they hum over a prayer also about sunrise in the morning.

—THOMAS FORSYTH, 1827

W hat do we look back on and count as the end of the year draws nearer—the hard things, the sorrows, the opportunities? Most likely the year brought a little bit of each to us. We may have experienced hurt—some deeper than we expected, some that still hurts—but if we tell ourselves that no weapon formed against us shall prosper, we will overcome it all.

As the New Year approaches, remember that although we may be no match for the troubles that we encounter, our angels are. It is our responsibility to speak for what is right, and then we let the ministering angels carry the ball. Their purpose is to help us, and our purpose is to give thanks and sing rather than cry.

Never let anybody be in a position to puzzle you in regard to what is right.

—WINNEBAGO

At times we are given a task that makes us wonder how qualified we are to complete it. Do we have what it takes, or should we hope for a miracle? When we are given something to do, we are given the tools to do it as well—not just personal expertise, but a faith in something beyond ourselves. As we draw on the courage that the Spirit gives, ideas flow and we can do anything. We gain the strength we need as we go—it doesn't just come magically. Our strength builds slowly as we move ahead in faith and hope. It is never just hope but absolute expectation. If we expect something, we get it.

You go too fast. No good to go so fast.

—HE BEAR, CHEYENNE

DECEMBER 29

L ike the trees that thrive along a moist ravine, we naturally grow stronger where we receive the best nourishment. All of us have our individual needs and, with the Spirit as our guide, we seek whatever nourishes those needs. Sometimes we get confused about what our true needs are, but the Spirit does not. That's why it's important to take time each day for quiet, Spirit time. Listen carefully and the Spirit will guide you to what you most deeply need.

You ask me to dig for stone! Shall I dig under her [the earth's] skin for her bones? Then when I die I can not enter her body to be born again.

—CHIEF SMOHALLA, WANAPUM

DECEMBER 30

What age are you? We can measure our age in years or in attitude. Some people with the most years are the youngest in attitude; some who are young in years are very old. But if we have an "old" attitude, can we change? You bet. Looking for help? Do it yourself. Take the bull by the horns and be your own best friend. Press in closer to that Almighty Spirit who gives life. Remember—age is just a word unless you lose interest in living.

Nobody knows when we die, maybe tomorrow or ten years.

—QUANAH PARKER, COMANCHE

DECEMBER 31

In life we experience brokenness, woundedness, and weakness. But take heart, life also offers healing. By living fully in the Spirit, we become stronger, more resilient, and more open to the healing that the Spirit continually offers.

As this year comes to an end and another year begins, remember to be as gentle with yourself and others as you would with the most fragile flower. Be honest but with kindness. Determine what causes pain and seek healing. Erase dark thoughts, and stand free and whole again. That is the gift the Spirit offers each new day, each new year. Claim it with anticipation, hope, and joy that you may live life in all abundance.

The Indian believes that the sun is a gift from God, our Father above, to enlighten the world and as the sun appears over the horizon they offer up a prayer in acceptance of our Father's gift.

—WASHAKIE, SHOSHONE

INDEX

ABOUT THE AUTHOR

Joyce Sequichie Hifler is the bestselling author of *A Cherokee Feast of Days*, *A Cherokee Feast of Days, Volume II* (a finalist for the national Books for a Better Life Award), *Think on These Things*, and *When the Night Bird Sings* as well as writing the nationally syndicated newspaper column, also titled "Think on These Things." Descended from the Sequichie family, who were marched to Oklahoma over the Trail of Tears, Hifler was recently inducted into the Indian Territory Hall of Fame. She lives with her husband of twenty-nine years in Bartlesville, Oklahoma.